Preserving Useful Knowledge

Preserving Useful Knowledge

A History of Collections Care at the APS Library

Renée Wolcott

American Philosophical Society Press
Philadelphia

Transactions of the
American Philosophical Society
Held at Philadelphia
for Promoting Useful Knowledge
Volume 111, Part 1

ISBN: 978-1-60618-113-3
Ebook ISBN: 978-1-60618-118-8
U.S. ISSN: 0065-9746

Library of Congress Cataloging-in-Publication Data

Names: Wolcott, Renée, 1960- author.
Title: Preserving useful knowledge : a history of collections care at the
   APS library / Renée Wolcott.
Description: Philadelphia : American Philosophical Society Press, [2022] |
   Series: Transactions of the American Philosophical Society Held at
   Philadelphia for Promoting Useful Knowledge, 0065-9746 ; volume 111,
   part 1 | Includes index.
Identifiers: LCCN 2022022773 | ISBN 9781606181133 (paperback)
Subjects: LCSH: Library materials—Conservation and restoration. |
   Bookbinding—Repairing. | Museum conservation methods. |
   American Philosophical Society. Library—History.
Classification: LCC Z701 .W65 2022 | DDC 025.8/4--dc23/eng/20220719
LC record available at https://lccn.loc.gov/2022022773s

Contents

Acknowledgments

Like many projects conceived just before the global outbreak of the novel coronavirus in 2019, this one followed an unusual course. I began the research for this book in December 2019, in preparation for a paper I had committed to delivering at the 48th Annual Meeting of the American Institute for Conservation in the summer of 2020. As fate would have it, I barely had the chance to begin examining the archives of the American Philosophical Society (APS) before the pandemic brought on-site library research to a screeching halt. Spending the next three months at home, however, gave me the opportunity to examine the digitized pages of the Society's earliest minute books and to begin piecing together its approach to collections care in the late eighteenth and early nineteenth centuries. I also transcribed William Berwick's correspondence with APS Librarian I. Minis Hays from the early twentieth century. When the APS Library reopened to staff in summer 2020, I spent additional time combing through the physical archives for evidence related to bookbinding and restoration in the late nineteenth and twentieth centuries. The book you hold in your hands is an expanded version of the paper I delivered at the virtual 2020 meeting of the American Institute for Conservation, revised for a broader audience.

The uneven course of the project was smoothed by many friends and colleagues, all of whom have my undying gratitude. Mary McDonald, then Head of Publications at the APS, suggested the book project that prompted further research into the history of conservation at the Society (*Art, Science, Invention: Conservation and the Peale-Sellers Family Collection*, published in the 2019 *Transactions of the American Philosophical Society*). Madalina Veres's extensive archival research for her 2008 timeline of the APS provided a firm foundation for further inquiry into the history of conservation. Paper conservator Christine Smith was incredibly helpful in securing image permissions and providing additional information about William Berwick and his work. Several conservation colleagues—particularly book conservator Giselle Simon and paintings conservator Joyce Hill Stoner—provided excellent suggestions for revision. David Gary, Associate

Director of Collections; Anne Downey, Head of Conservation; and Anisha Gupta, then Assistant Conservator at the APS, provided endless support and encouragement. APS Executive Officer Bob Hauser provided wise and generous leadership during the pandemic.

Introduction

In the early twentieth century, art conservators such as George Stout of Harvard University's Fogg Art Museum used physical examination and analytical techniques to determine how works of art were made and how their materials reacted to the environment over time. While artists' materials and techniques remain an important focus for conservation research today, conservators also recognize the imperative to document their own history of engagement with artifacts. As the field—a blend of chemistry, art history, and hand–eye skills—enters its second century, scholars increasingly recognize the importance of recording the motivating philosophies, materials, and techniques employed by binders, restorers, and conservation trailblazers. Kenneth E. Harris and Susan E. Schur of the Library of Congress have authored "A Brief History of Preservation and Conservation at the Library of Congress," which covers the same time period that I document here.[1] Book conservator Saira Haqqi has researched and recorded early twentieth-century rebinding practices at the Morgan Library.[2] In its humble way, this book joins more ambitious endeavors such as Sheila Waters' *Waters Rising*, which describes Peter Waters' efforts to preserve Italian books and manuscripts damaged in the Florence flood of 1966, and Ellen Cunningham-Kruppa's *Mooring a Field*, which traces the development of graduate programs in book and paper conservation.[3] This book looks at the long history of collections care at the American Philosophical Society, a learned society whose inception predates the American Revolution.

The APS has maintained a research library since its founding in 1743. In the institution's 275-year history, the Library's approach to collections

---

[1] Kenneth E. Harris and Susan E. Schur, "A Brief History of Preservation and Conservation at the Library of Congress," www.loc.gov/preservation/about/history/pres-hist.pdf.

[2] Saira Haqqi, "The Rationale for Rebinding at the Pierpont Morgan Library in the Early 20th-Century: A Study of Bindings by Marguerite Duprez Lahey," *Book and Paper Group Annual* 35 (2016), 17–29.

[3] Sheila Waters, *Waters Rising: Letters from Florence* (Ann Arbor, MI: The Legacy Press, 2016) and Ellen Cunningham-Kruppa, *Mooring a Field: Paul N. Banks and the Education of Library and Archives Conservators* (Ann Arbor, MI: The Legacy Press, 2019).

care has changed as the conservation field has evolved, from binding loose documents and pamphlets in the 1700s to the professional repair of books and manuscripts in today's fully staffed and well-equipped conservation lab. In the years between, the APS forged relationships with many contract binders and restorers beyond its walls and eventually established its own in-house conservation facility.

The APS Archives reveal the Library's long-standing concern with stabilizing its collections and provide details concerning the individuals hired to perform the work, including Philadelphia binder Jane Aitken in the early nineteenth century; Library of Congress manuscript restorer William Berwick in the early twentieth century; Carol Rugh (later Carolyn Horton), who was hired as the first APS on-site conservator in 1935; and Willman Spawn, the Society's first full-time conservator in 1960. Not all of these restorers and conservators left records of their work, but the collections themselves reflect the changing materials and methods in use over the years, including Western-paper fills and silk lamination, indiscriminate rebinding, and today's historically sensitive item-level treatment.

This long, varied history of collections care means that today's conservators—trained in graduate programs dedicated to art conservation—must sometimes reverse earlier treatments that no longer serve the needs of the books and documents they were designed to protect. This constant engagement with and reassessment of conservation work from the past is common in smaller research libraries, particularly as scientific conservation techniques have been slower to catch on in the complex interplay among binders, restorers, and program-trained book conservators. This book discusses the evolution of conservation treatment at the APS and its conservators' present approach to items that require repeated repair.

As conservators increasingly engage not only with unaltered works of art, books, and archival collections, but also with the treatment materials of their predecessors, documentation of historic conservation practices is vital to finding an ethical path forward. Our treatment decisions must take into consideration the multi-layered histories of the objects in our care, as well as the past, present, and future stewards of our cultural heritage.

CHAPTER 1

1743–1846: Early History of the APS Collections and Their Care

When polymath Benjamin Franklin (1706–1790) founded the American Philosophical Society for the "pursuit of useful knowledge," he brought together a small group of men who studied the latest developments in science and agriculture in order to promote the welfare of the American colonies. These men read and collected books and papers on the latest scientific discoveries, exchanged botanical and mineralogical specimens, and established ties with scholars in other parts of the world. In December 1768, the American Philosophical Society merged with another small society with similar aims, The American Society held at Philadelphia for Promoting Useful Knowledge. The books, papers, and specimens of both societies were brought together, and by 1770 one of the main goals of the enlarged Society was to maintain a Cabinet—a research library and museum—worthy of international acclaim. The committees of the expanded society, and its growing library, focused on geography, mathematics, natural philosophy, and astronomy; medicine and anatomy; natural history and chemistry; trade and commerce; mechanics and architecture; and husbandry and American improvements. In the last decades of the eighteenth century, the Society's Cabinet contained donated and purchased reference books, papers submitted to the Society, and meeting minutes as well as natural history specimens, medals, and architectural and mechanical models.

The APS Minutes from this period reveal the Society's concern with the security and preservation of its growing collections.[4] The Society

---

[4] Unless otherwise stated, references pertaining to the early history of the APS are taken from the *Minutes of the American Philosophical Library* from 1769 to 1846 in the APS Archives. These are available online through the APS digital library (https://diglib.amphilsoc.org/islandora /graphics/minutes-american-philosophical-society). Page numbers for each citation are given in the text.

purchased a new bookcase for its Library in 1773, when its Members met in rented space in Carpenters' Hall, and more cases were added as the collections continued to expand. Astronomer David Rittenhouse (1732–1796, see page 44) was appointed the first APS Librarian in 1775, charged with overseeing the Society's collections and monitoring its lending practices. From 1783 to 1790, while the Society struggled to purchase land and erect a building after the Revolutionary War, Rittenhouse stored the APS Library and Museum collections in his own home. Printed ownership labels were pasted into the books and pamphlets during this period. The collections moved into the newly constructed Philosophical Hall in early 1790 (see fig. 1). In 1792, the Society established regulations for the management of the Library, including cataloguing guidelines, lending restrictions, and fines for overdue books. The Society's Curators were to use the proceeds from any fines for the "augmenting of their Library, & keeping the same in proper preservation" (222).

According to the APS Minutes, Society Members first called for the Library collections to be catalogued in 1790, when the books were moved to their new home, but the process took years to complete. In early 1793, all of the loaned books were recalled from borrowers for the purposes of creating the catalogue. When artist Charles Willson Peale (1741–1827) rented part of the Society's hall for his museum in 1794, he was named Librarian of the Society and given the responsibility of caring for both the collections and the building. Along with two other APS Members, he presented a draft of the Library catalogue in 1796. Discussions for printing the catalogue were underway in 1797, and the Society moved on to cataloguing its "cabinet of minerals" and "mathematical and philosophical apparatus" (170). The Library catalogue project appears to have stalled, however, perhaps because books kept disappearing. Although unauthorized borrowing or outright theft is not addressed directly in the APS Minutes, a committee was directed "to take proper measures to secure the property in the Society Room" in November 1798 (233), and locks were installed on the bookcases before the next meeting. New bookcases with glazing were installed the following year to assist with the cataloguing process. The catalogue was finally completed in December 1799, and the books were grouped by size and numbered sequentially. This catalogue was revised from 1807 to 1814; in 1819 (by which time the collection had again outgrown its bookcases); from 1822 to 1824; in 1838, when the Society also purchased a stamp for marking

Figure 1. Philosophical Hall, which contained the APS meeting rooms and Library, after its construction in 1790. APS Archives, unprocessed collection, M42.34.25. Courtesy of the American Philosophical Society.

the books; and in the early 1860s, when the catalogue was first organized as a series of card files. Lists of book donations—and the ever-increasing costs for insuring the Library collections—reflect the growing size and importance of the APS holdings during this period.

Binding as Collections Care

From the invention of the codex in the fourth century of the current era through the end of the hand-binding period in the nineteenth century, bookbinders and related artisans such as scribes and illuminators were responsible for repairing dilapidated books. The convenient format of the bound volume has its weaknesses, especially at all of the points of flexion: the joints between the covers and spine, the interaction between the paper leaves and the system used for sewing them, and the spine itself. These areas became weaker as book production became more rapid, and the heavy, over-engineered bindings of the medieval period became more lightweight, more attenuated, and easier to execute. Through the mid-nineteenth century, book collectors routinely hired binders to rebind books whose spines were missing or whose cover boards were detached. This process generally included replacing the original covering material (usually leather over wooden or paper boards) with new material, and either adding new endleaves to the text block or mending the hinges between the new cover and the older interior. Binders might also replace the spine material alone, either by inserting new leather beneath the old (a process known as rebacking) or by adhering new leather on top of the old (a process known as overbacking). Artists might be hired for more specialized restorations, such as recreating lost portions of illuminated manuscripts, but this was far less common. Like its peers, the Society's Library relied heavily on bookbinders during its first century of existence.

    Binding loose papers provides protection against both mishandling and loss, and it appears to have become a standard procedure during the early days of the Society's Library. As part of the process of preparing the first catalogue of the Library collections, the Society ordered in March 1797 "that the pamphlets belonging to the Society be arranged and uniformly bound" (160) and in November 1799 that all the unbound books in the Society's possession be bound. On October 15, 1802, the APS Minutes note that an incoming donation of quartos from another learned society "being unbound [will] be bound" (129). A year later, APS Members were not permitted to borrow the latest or "loose" journals (170), suggesting that the Library's usual practice was to bind sets of journals on a regular basis. According to the Society's financial records, Philadelphia printer Robert Aitken (1734–1802) and his daughter, Jane Aitken (1764–1832), served as two of the Society's earliest binders.[5] Robert Desilver (or De Silver), another Philadelphia publisher, took over the binding work after Jane Aitken's second bankruptcy in 1814, and he continued binding tracts and journals for the Society until 1822.

Starting in 1821, the APS Librarian (then wine merchant and philanthropist John Vaughan, see fig. 2) was given an appropriation for binding each year, starting at $50 and rising to $200 annually by 1844. During this period, when first Vaughan (1756–1841) and then naturalist George Ord (1781–1866) served as the Society's Librarians, the collection of the Library grew enormously, through book purchases, donations, and exchanges with other learned societies. Many of these books and serial publications required binding, and the Society's archives are rich in receipts and other financial records for the binders used for this routine work, including Benjamin Gaskill (1786–1859, active 1821–1852), Jacob Snider (active 1831–1836), Jacob's son George Snider (active 1836–1842), and Edward Gaskill (active 1852–1854). Each of these binders bound hundreds of journals, pamphlets, and reference works for the Society. Other binders were occasionally hired for special work, including George P. Story, who bound Peter Stephen DuPonceau's dissertation on Chinese writing in 1938, and C. Carle, who bound John James Audubon's *Birds of America* in 1840 (the binding was subscribed by Audubon himself, who became an APS Member in 1831).

Although the annual binding appropriation covered the routine binding of printed materials, the Society also bound many of its manuscript collections, including its own archival records. On November 17, 1837, the APS Secretaries were instructed "to cause the Records and Documents, connected with the History and Transactions of the Society, to be properly arranged and bound" and installed in appropriate cases (174). This directive was carried out by February 19, 1841, when J. Francis Fisher, the APS

---

[5] Information about the Society's binders is taken from the APS Archives, which contain the Society's treasurers' accounts, binding orders, and miscellaneous papers and receipts.

Figure 2. John Vaughan (1756–1841), a Philadelphia wine merchant, served as APS Librarian from 1803 until his death in 1841. The first printed catalogue of the APS Library was produced under his aegis, and he also donated many valuable books. Thomas Sully's 1823 portrait depicts Vaughan holding an APS book with a torn parchment binding propped on a copy of the Library's catalogue. Thomas Sully, *Portrait of John Vaughan*, 1823. Oil on canvas. 40.25 × 35 inches. Courtesy of the American Philosophical Society.

Member who organized the papers, announced that they had been bound into "eighteen quarto, and two folio volumes which seem neatly and sufficiently well executed by our Binder Mr. [George] Snider, who has taken great pains with them."[6] According to various treasurers' accounts, Snider received $48.50 from the General Fund of the Society for this work.

On October 21, 1842, naturalist and APS Librarian George Ord "called the attention of the Society to the condition of the bound manuscripts in the Library, some of which are without indices, and parts of others have been cut out of the volumes which once contained them, and have been removed" (294). A committee was appointed "to consider the Manuscripts in the possession or custody of the Society . . . [and to report] . . . what action may be proper for their secure preservation, and for facilitating their usefulness" (295). This approach also appears to have involved binding or rebinding, although the APS Minutes do not specify what was done; the committee was disbanded in August 1845.

Not all of the Society's manuscript collections were dealt with so speedily. The APS Minutes of July 17, 1840, note that "[Charles Pemberton] Fox had deposited in their archives a collection of papers and original letters of Dr. Franklin" (57). The following month, the Society appointed a committee "to arrange the Franklin papers deposited with the Society, and to report a plan for the better preservation of the Manuscripts of the Society" (62). The efforts of this committee appear to have lapsed, because the APS Minutes of November 2, 1849, show that Franklin's great-grandson Dr. Franklin Bache (1792–1864) passed a resolution calling for a new committee to "consider of the best means of arranging and preserving the 'Franklin Manuscript Papers' now in possession of this Society" (225). The resulting committee comprised Bache, former APS Librarian George Ord, and the current APS Librarian Charles B. Trego (1794–1874), a geologist, who was given additional funding to sort the papers, arrange them chronologically, and index them in preparation for binding. Trego did not receive his final payment for the task until a few days after Bache's death in 1864, when he collected a final $70 from the General Fund for arranging and indexing fifty-seven volumes of Franklin papers. In the same year, the Society paid its routine binders, the Philadelphia firm of Pawson & Nicholson, $245.82:

---

[6] J. Francis Fisher to Franklin Bache, February 19, 1841, APS Archives, Record Group IId.

more than three times the sixty-odd dollars usually disbursed for binding each year. As restorer William Berwick's later correspondence reveals, this investment only paid for the cheapest sort of binding; the loose Franklin letters were merely oversewn (whipstitched together into sections) and bound, without any new paper added at the spine edges to protect the original letters from glue.

Other Early Preservation Efforts

Although care for the Library collections appears to have focused on binding during the eighteenth and nineteenth centuries, the Society was also interested in preserving its instruments, natural history specimens, and artworks from harm, and in repairing them when they were damaged. On April 4, 1783, the curators presented a "report on the state of the natural curiosities in the Museum," and the Society "ordered that the curators take immediate measures for preserving the same from further decay" (n.p.). Based on these records and the letters of Charles Willson Peale, proprietor of the Philadelphia Museum, it is wise to assume that any skins and taxidermied specimens then in the APS collections were treated with arsenic, mercury, or other toxic materials during that time. In early 1802, the Society considered several options for repairing and maintaining its timepiece. On June 18, 1802, the curators were "requested to put the Lens [of the telescope] in good order & have the globes varnished with spirit varnish and properly covered" (126). On June 17, 1836, the Society turned its attention to repairing its "transit instruments" (109), which had been used to observe the transit of Venus across the face of the sun. Franklin's portrait was "cleaned and repaired" for the sum of $28 in 1842 (30). All of this information is valuable for today's conservators, who may be called on to re-treat instruments, specimens, or paintings that were first restored more than 150 years ago. At other institutions as well, the archives may fill in some of the blanks concerning restoration work undertaken before the age of modern conservation documentation.

The APS Archives also provide tantalizing clues concerning the early study of preservation and the development of new materials and technologies. The Society actively collected information related to preservation, and it conducted its own research on the matter. On March 20, 1789, the APS Minutes record the donation of a dissertation in French on protecting paper from the ravages of insects. On February 16, 1798, a committee of three was appointed "to devise the best method of preserving fossil bones" as they were raised from the ground (210). On January 17, 1806, an Italian pamphlet was criticized for containing "nothing of importance, except a mode of preserving books from worms, which simply consists in mixing oil of turpentine with the paste used in binding—which, in drying, the writer says, forms a vitreous substance with the paste" (37). The APS Minutes also reflect its Members' interest in mulberry paper from American trees, the development of machine-made paper in 1819 (Josiah and Thomas Gilpin's "endless sheet" [98]), methods for shaping caoutchouc, early daguerre-otypes and other photographic techniques, the first metal-nib pens, and experiments to develop a sediment-free ink for such pens.

CHAPTER 2

Restoration and Conservation from the Twentieth Century to the Present

Although the APS continued to employ binders in the latter half of the nineteenth century, its librarians were no doubt facing the issues that prompted rapid changes in the protection and repair of books and manuscripts over the next century: chemically unstable original materials such as brittle inks, papers, and leathers; damage associated with frequent handling and overcrowded conditions; and threats from light, heat, pests, fire, water, and other environmental intrusions. Increased literacy and changes brought about by the Industrial Revolution meant that libraries were eagerly collecting both books and manuscripts from the hand-binding period and modern materials produced using the latest technological advances in binding, papermaking, and ink production. By the turn of the twentieth century, libraries were specifically concerned by the longevity of manuscripts written in iron gall ink, as well as changes observed in modern paper and leather.

Problems with iron gall ink—which can cause brittleness, cracking, and holes in inked paper—were already well known by the late nineteenth century. The ink was used from the medieval period until synthetic dyes were invented, and its use for some government documents persisted into the mid-twentieth century. Even though the black ink often becomes dark brown over time, it was preferred for legal documents because it etches permanently into the surface to which it is applied, making it hard to erase. The chemistry of iron gall ink was poorly understood in the early twentieth century, but we now know that the ferrous sulfate and gallotannic acids that give the ink its rich black color also make it acidic, and the ink's metallic components often catalyze corrosion or oxidation of the underlying paper. Librarians of the time were eager to find strong, transparent materials for reinforcing iron gall ink manuscripts, particularly those that were written on both sides. Loss of the inked components could otherwise make an informative document into an illegible piece of paper lace.

The Industrial Revolution had also given rise to modern library materials that aged far more rapidly than their historic counterparts. Papers based on wood pulp rather than linen or cotton rags were also acidic, and the papers quickly became brown and brittle regardless of the inks used on them. Leathers produced using fast-acting synthetic tanning agents rather than the lengthy, arduous, and smelly traditional procedures for tanning were similarly acidic and quick to deteriorate, becoming orange-red, dusty, and weak (a condition now known as red rot). Developments such as gas lights, which contributed to sulfur-based air pollution, exacerbated the damage to both paper and leather.

Problems like these (which continue to spur the development of new conservation treatments even today) led to rapid changes in the field that is now known as art conservation. In the late nineteenth century, chemists began working closely with librarians and art historians to better understand how artworks, archival manuscripts, and printed books were made and to explicate the forces by which they deteriorated. Although artists and craftspeople had always repaired or "restored" works of art (often by adding new material to compensate for damage to original materials), advances in analytical chemistry offered twentieth-century restorers a way to understand how artworks had been restored in the past and which new materials were safe to use in the future. In the early- to mid-twentieth century, libraries and museums began dedicating space and staff to scientific collections care.

Looting and destruction of European cultural heritage during World War II and the Florence Flood of 1966, which damaged so many of Italy's libraries and archives, focused the attention of the nascent preservation field on the need for standardized, well-researched treatment methods. In the United States, the term "conservation" began to be used to describe repair work informed by chemistry, materials analysis, and a code of ethics that prioritized documentation, reversible treatment methods, and the retention of original materials. Scientific and ethical considerations distinguished "conservation" from "restoration," or repair work that merely sought to return an object to wholeness. When graduate programs in art conservation were established in the United States in the 1960s and 1970s, they taught technical analysis along with the hand skills required to repair works of art.[7]

For graduates of these programs, who call themselves "conservators," "restoration" has dual and sometimes contradictory meanings. It can be used to describe informed treatment work that goes beyond physical and chemical stabilization (the goals of "conservation" treatment) to return an object—a book, painting, sculpture, or document—either to its original appearance or to its appearance at a specific point in its history. But it can also be used in a negative sense, to describe repair work that is not guided by the latest scientific research or by ethical considerations. Although conservation work should always be documented and detectible, restoration work in the latter sense may not be. Unscrupulous dealers who wish to pass off a repaired artifact as a pristine, undamaged work of art rely on this type of restoration. Such work may destroy historical evidence, utilize materials or methods that will speed the object's deterioration, or—if the treatment is not reversible—prevent the use of improved repair methods when better materials or techniques are developed.[8] Clients who seek to have their treasures repaired should be aware of both senses of the word and ensure that the person performing the treatment—whether billed as a conservator or a restorer—will meet their desiderata when it comes to procedural documentation, reversibility, retention of original elements, and chemical stability of repair materials.[9]

Preservation and the APS Library Building

Although conservation treatment focuses on the repair of damaged artifacts, it is only part of the larger goal of preserving all of a library or museum's collections. Preservation goals include protecting books and

---

[7] For a brief history of art conservation in the twentieth century, see Joyce Hill Stoner, "Changing Approaches in Art Conservation: 1925 to the Present," in *Scientific Examination of Art: Modern Techniques in Conservation and Analysis* (Washington, DC: The National Academies Press, 2005), 40–57.

[8] It should be noted that "restoration" and "conservation" are synonymous in the United Kingdom and Europe, where practitioners are often known as "conservator-restorers." The United States art conservation community is alone in drawing a distinction between the terms, and their definitions are still being debated.

[9] Art conservators or restorers who are worthy of their titles adhere to the American Institute for Conservation Code of Ethics, which can be found online at www.culturalheritage.org /about-conservation/code-of-ethics.

manuscripts from excessive light, heat, moisture, fire, pollution, pests, theft, and loss. Although policies and procedures can be put into place that minimize these risks, the library building itself is the primary form of protection for the materials it contains. Its insulation, ventilation, lighting, and other building systems play the leading role in keeping collections safe. Although conservators are trained in the hands-on repair of various types of materials, they are also trained to work with facilities staff, building engineers, and emergency responders to prevent damage to the collections on a larger scale.

The APS Library remained in Philosophical Hall throughout the late nineteenth century, but its collections were rapidly outgrowing the space. A blind third floor with a clerestory was added on top of Philosophical Hall in 1890 purely to house the books and manuscripts. This extra floor spoiled the Federal style of the building and was derogatively likened to an ugly top hat, but it remained in place until construction of Independence National Historical Park in 1949 (see figs. 3 and 4). The Library's rarest materials were shipped from this space to restorer William Berwick in Washington, DC, and returned again by express shipping services such as American Express (see page 19).

In 1934, the Society finally acquired additional space in the Drexel Building, a towering bank headquarters built across the street from Philosophical Hall in the late 1880s (see fig. 5). One of the benefits of moving the Library's special collections to the Drexel Building may have been the availability of fireproof vaults. In 1929, the published Minutes of the Meetings of the APS reflect a growing concern not only with the overcrowded conditions in Philosophical Hall but with the lack of protection from fire and theft:

> The Library Committee wishes to call the attention of the Society as a whole to the inadequate protection from fire or theft of its priceless collection of Manuscripts and Books and to urge that the Society take action at as early a date as possible, to provide more adequate protection for these treasures, the loss of which would be irreparable.[10]

Securing the Library's collections evidently involved both locating a safer space for its materials and hiring its first on-site restorer, Carol Rugh, to assess and repair the materials (see page 25).

---

[10] "Minutes of the Meetings of the American Philosophical Society during 1929," *Proceedings of the American Philosophical Society* 68, no. 1 (1929): xii.

Figure 3. Philosophical Hall after its 1890 renovation, which added a blind third floor with a clerestory to house the APS Library collections. Print Collection, graphics:9588. Courtesy of the American Philosophical Society.

Two succeeding generations of part-time conservators—Helen A. Price (see page 31) and Willman Spawn (see page 32)—also worked in the Drexel Building in the 1940s and 1950s. Shortly after he was hired in 1948, Spawn assisted with two collections moves as nineteenth-century buildings made way for a re-envisioned Old City and today's Independence National

Figure 4. The library on the third floor of Philosophical Hall in 1947, when many of the Library's holdings had already been moved to the Drexel Building across the street. APS Archives, Negative no. 9. Courtesy of the American Philosophical Society.

Historical Park.[11] In 1952, the Drexel Building was slated for demolition, and the APS moved quickly to draft plans for a new Library Hall on the same site. In keeping with the bicentennial fervor then sweeping the city, the hall's exterior would reproduce the 1790 Library Company building previously erected there. In the interim, Spawn helped to transfer the APS collections to the United States Fidelity and Guaranty Company Building.

The old-on-the-outside, new-on-the-inside Library Hall was completed in 1959, and Spawn moved the collections once again in 1960. APS Librarian Richard H. Shryock (1893–1972) described the new space in the

---

[11] Unless otherwise stated, information about Willman Spawn comes from the Foundation for Advancement in Conservation (FAIC) oral history interview with him and his wife, Carol Spawn, conducted by Julie Baker on April 24, 2004. FAIC Oral History Files, Winterthur Museum, Library, and Archives.

Figure 5.   The APS Library as housed in the Drexel Building, from an undated photograph. Prints Collection, graphics:9594. Courtesy of the American Philosophical Society.

Proceedings of the American Philosophical Society and included floor plans of the building, which featured stacks with room for growth, air conditioning, and a small "restoration laboratory" on the second floor. "The air-conditioning will minister to the comfort of the staff and simultaneously to the more effective preservation of books and manuscripts," Shryock wrote.[12]

As all research librarians know, there is never enough room to grow. By 1985, the Society's collections had already outgrown Library Hall. The Society purchased the former Farmers' and Mechanics' Bank Building at 427 Chestnut Street and renovated it to include storage for its non-rare books, as well as an auditorium and an enlarged conservation laboratory. The three floors of stacks in that building (now known as Benjamin Franklin Hall) are now nearing capacity, and the lower levels of Library

---

[12] Richard H. Shryock, "The Planning and Formal Opening of Library Hall," *Proceedings of the American Philosophical Society* 104, no. 4 (1960): 356.

Hall were renovated in 2021 to accommodate compact shelving. After 250 years, the search for more space, more security, and better environmental controls continues.

Commercial Binding, Repair, and Rebinding

Commercial binding and book repair continued unabated at the APS throughout the twentieth century, even as the Library turned to trained restorers and conservators for some of its preservation efforts.[13] While restorer William Berwick—himself a trained binder—was hired to disbind and mend the Society's most important manuscripts in the early twentieth century (see page 19), the restored Franklin, Lee, and Greene papers were returned to Philadelphia to be rebound by commercial binders Pawson & Nicholson (1848–1911) or by Hyman Zucker, a Pawson & Nicholson employee who established his own bindery when the larger firm closed. Zucker continued to work for the APS—singly or as part of Zucker & Henckel—until 1947. In addition to routine journal and pamphlet binding, these binders also resewed and rebacked damaged volumes, inserted plates, repaired manuscripts and newspapers, pressed cockled paper, and mended and mounted maps. Both binderies produced well-made half or three-quarter leather volumes, often in red morocco; Zucker penciled his name and the binding's cost on the back pastedown of each book.

Between 1900 and Carol Rugh's hire as a part-time book conservator in 1935 (see page 25), the Society used at least nine Philadelphia bookbinders, including Eickhoff & Kraemer, J. B. Lippincott, F. W. Eickhoff, Albert Oldach, E. C. Groschupf, and Messrs. Smith and Fehr. Although some of these binders focused purely on binding journals, pamphlets, or reference books, others also repaired books and maps. In fact, Rugh's admirable approach to conservation was likely developed during her tenure with Albert Oldach, who was an experienced restorer as well as a fine binder.

After 1947, when both Fehr and Zucker went out of business, the Society's only remaining binder appears to have been Savidge & Krimmel. Whereas the earlier binders worked to specification in cloth and leather, Savidge & Krimmel was advertised as a "library binding service." Like many late twentieth-century library binderies, the firm probably cut the spines

---

[13] Details on the commercial binders employed by the Society come from the binding orders in Series VII.6.c. of the American Philosophical Society Archives.

from books with a guillotine to avoid the labor-intensive process of dis-binding them. The resulting pile of loose leaves would then be oversewn and glued into a stiff buckram case. Library bindings like these open poorly and are devoid of historical context. Some of the Library's earliest printed books, including William Cowley's 1758 *Illustration and Mensuration of Solid Geometry* and a copy of Benjamin Rush's 1794 *An Account of the Bilious Remitting Yellow Fever*, received this treatment in the twentieth century, and any original bindings they may have had are now lost. Of the fourteen Savidge & Krimmel binding order books in the APS Archives, two (both dated after 1961) are dedicated solely to rebinding.

The primacy of the text, coupled with a disregard for the material culture of historic bindings, is clearly illustrated throughout the Society's second century, but the Library Committee and Library staff were not consistent in their approach. In the 1940s, restorer Helen A. Price was hired specifically to care for the Society's dilapidated leather bindings. By the 1960s, Willman Spawn—who treated thousands of the Society's dis-bound manuscripts—was struggling to hide similar leather-bound books in the APS collections for fear they would be sent to Fritz and Trudi Eberhardt or Savidge & Krimmel for rebinding. This erratic regard for early and orig-inal bindings is a cause for dismay among today's conservators and book historians, who can glean a great deal of contextual information from how a book was originally bound. Further research may be able to establish which of the Library's earliest bindings—by the likes of Jane Aitken and Benjamin Gaskill—remain intact.

1900–1920: *William Berwick (1848–1920), Paper Restorer*

In 1900, the APS hired expert paper restorer William Berwick (see fig. 6) to again address its collections pertaining to Benjamin Franklin, Thomas Jefferson, Nathanael Greene, and other luminaries of the early republic. Berwick's hire—as the first professional restorer known to be employed by the Society—coincided with new breakthroughs in library preservation, such as the use of thin silk gauze or crepeline to line brittle manuscripts. His selection as a practitioner of this new technology demonstrates the Society's dedication to preserving its collections. Berwick's professional ca-reer and the conservation developments surrounding it have been expertly

Figure 6.   William Berwick at work, circa 1916. Courtesy of the William Berwick Family Collection.

covered by paper conservator Christine Smith in her 2016 magnum opus; the following paragraphs owe much to her labors.[14]

Berwick was born in London on February 28, 1848, and apparently apprenticed as a bookbinder. He immigrated to Canada in or around 1866, and as a young man worked as a binder in Hamilton, Toronto, and Montreal. While in Montreal, he married Mary Gillespie, and by the time they immigrated to Lansing, Michigan, around 1882, they had two daughters, Mae and Edith. In Lansing, Berwick worked as a binder and restorer, repairing and mounting maps for the state land office. When his firm went out of business, he took the civil service exam, and in 1897 he applied successfully for a binding job at the U.S. Government Printing Office. He made his prior restoration experience known, and in 1899 he was assigned to the Division of Manuscripts in the Library of Congress on his birthday, at the age of fifty-one. He directed manuscript preservation at the Library of Congress until he died unexpectedly at his bench in 1920.

In addition to his full-time work at the Library of Congress, Berwick took on vast quantities of contractual work for other employers, including the American Philosophical Society, the New York State Library, and the State Historical Society of Wisconsin. His correspondence with I. Minis Hays (1847–1925), the ophthalmologist and APS Member who served as Society Librarian from 1897 to 1922, reveals that Berwick often dedicated evenings, weekends, holidays, and vacations to his private work, possibly (as Smith notes) because his pay from the Government Printing Office was so low.[15] Berwick's constant concern—still familiar to modern conservators—was maintaining a steady supply of high-quality materials for his work. Many of his letters to Hays focus on procuring silk crepeline, tracing cloth of the proper color and thickness for use in book repair, and antique papers to be used for fills and false margins. In one early letter to Hays, he wrote, "Often I come across more flyleaves in a book than are wanted & so remove them, if you have any old books that can be treated thus I shall be

---

[14] Christine Smith, *Yours Respectfully, William Berwick: Paper Conservation in the United States and Western Europe, 1800 to 1935* (Ann Arbor, MI: The Legacy Press, 2016).

[15] Willman Spawn brought the Berwick-Hays correspondence to light during Christine Smith's first research trip to the APS around 1998. The APS Librarians at the time did not know the papers existed, and Spawn came out of retirement to show Smith where the boxes of correspondence were kept. Many of the APS Archives remain unprocessed to this day and may reveal more details about the institution's conservation history.

glad if you will attend to it for me."[16] Hays apparently followed through on this request at least once, as Berwick notes in a letter dated August 2, 1904:

> The few sheets you took out of the vols when I saw you last are gems in their line & it seems to me to be a crime to allow such paper to remain on shelves, so any time you may have to spare may be put to good use by removing some more & letting me have them. It seems to me that making paper as they did in those days is a lost art.

One wonders which books in the APS collections had their endleaves or blank pages sacrificed for Berwick's labors! Today's conservators would shrink from robbing one old book to repair another, as the number of blank endleaves in a given volume is a good indicator of the binding's original value.

Berwick began work on the Society's manuscripts in May 1900 and continued until his death in 1920. He started with the William Penn manuscripts and went on to treat other important APS collections, including the papers of Revolutionary-era statesman Richard Henry Lee; the early laws and provincial council minutes of Pennsylvania; the military correspondence of George Weedon; and Thomas Jefferson's muddy, tattered, moldy "Indian vocabularies" of Indigenous languages. The only printed work his letters refer to is a "Mercury newspaper," most likely Andrew Bradford's *American Weekly Mercury*, the first newspaper printed in the mid-Atlantic states, which ran from 1719 to 1749. Berwick's most monumental task, which engaged him for thirteen years, was conserving the Benjamin Franklin Papers, Mss.B.F85. This collection contained 13,284 items in fifty-seven bound volumes (which expanded to roughly 114 volumes after Berwick's treatment), and the expert restorer was rightly proud when he had finished.

The manuscripts had all been previously bound, and Berwick's treatment began with disbinding and separating the leaves, a task made more challenging by the poor condition of the documents and the time-saving practices of earlier binders. At least in the cases of the Franklin and Nathanael Greene papers, the binder or binders hired by the APS had sawn deeply into the spine edges of the letters and then oversewn them as groups of single sheets.[17] This both damaged the writing and allowed glue

---

[16] William Berwick to I. Minis Hays, October 31, 1900. Berwick-Hays correspondence, American Philosophical Society Archives.

[17] Although the Franklin manuscripts were almost certainly bound by the Philadelphia firm of Pawson & Nicholson in 1864, it is unclear who bound the Nathanael Greene papers. They may have been bound by Robert Desilver, who donated them to the APS in 1820.

to penetrate between the letters when the spine was lined and covered, as Berwick noted in his letters to Hays on October 31, 1900, and in August 1915, respectively:

> I have received the vol. of the Franklin papers & agree with you that they are in a <u>very bad condition</u> & will require time, very great care & <u>patience</u> to take apart. Letters that are bound in this way are always more difficult to take apart than a <u>folded</u> sheet for in this the glue only touches the outside of the fold, but in single sheets like those sent the glue finds its way in between each sheet & also onto the thread overcasting. I will however take great pains to preserve the mss.

> This Vol [5] of Greene letters is the worst bound Vol as yet, the binder ? has taken considerable pains to have deep saw marks & then let the glue run in, in many cases at least an inch making the task of taking it apart very difficult & then at the expense of many mutilated leaves.

> It is shameful the way these valuable documents have been treated. What surprises me is how your readers have managed to read the writing close to the back.

Berwick also pointed out that the former binders had often inserted leaves backward, with their outer or fore-edges bound into the gutter. He corrected these errors before returning the manuscripts. He was well aware that the treated documents were slated to be bound once more after their return to the APS (ironically, by Pawson & Nicholson), and he was eager to prevent further errors and damage after his extensive labor. His letters to Hays often offer advice for having the books rebound, stored, and handled, particularly when oversize folded manuscripts or maps needed to be bound in.

Berwick's conservation work to prepare the manuscripts for rebinding included removal of surface dirt (apparently using both dry and aqueous methods), flattening creases and re-sizing paper (coating it with a dilute adhesive to strengthen it), removing former mends and adhesives, adding new Western-paper fills and false margins (see fig. 7), and lining with paper and/or silk crepeline. The finished manuscripts were hinged to ledger paper with thin tracing cloth or bond paper. Berwick sometimes removed seals and replaced them in their original positions when the paper treatment was finished, and he inserted shields to prevent thick seals from damaging adjacent leaves. Occasionally, he also split manuscripts through their thickness, particularly when oversize double-sided sheets would have to be folded prior to rebinding, which would interrupt the flow of the text. In many cases, Berwick described his methods when returning the letters,

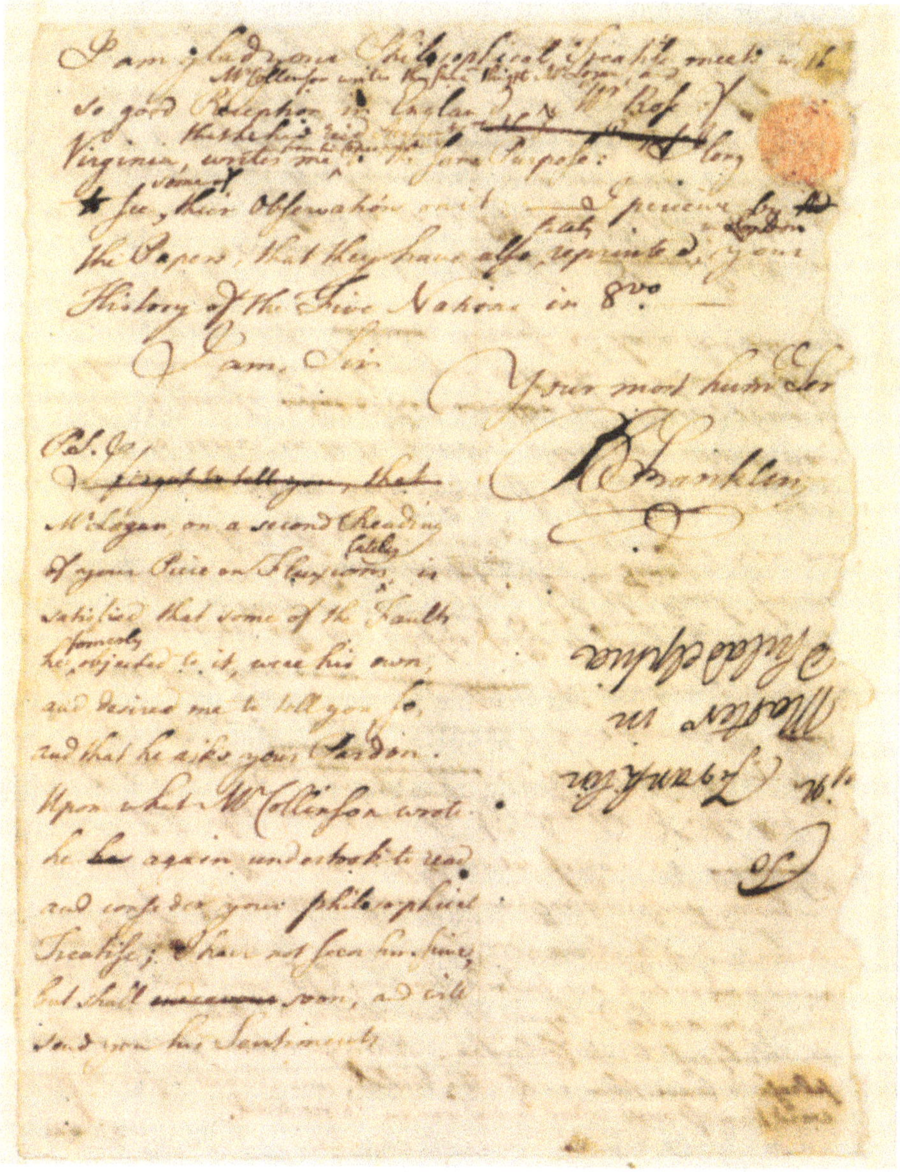
I am glad your Philosophical Treatise meets with
so good Reception in England
Virginia, writes me to the same Purpose:
I see their Observations and I perceive by the
the Papers, that they have also reprinted your
History of the Five Nations in 8vo.
I am, Sir
Your most humble Servt
B Franklin
P.S.
Mr Logan on a second Reading
of your Piece on Fluxions, is
satisfied that some of the Faults
he formerly objected to it, were his own,
and desired me to tell you so,
and that he asks your Pardon.
Upon what Mr Collinson wrote
he has again undertaken to read
and consider your philosophical
Treatise; I have not seen him since,
but shall soon, and will
send you his Sentiments.

Figure 7. William Berwick filled the losses in this letter, provided it with handling margins, and laminated it with silk sometime between 1900 and 1913. Benjamin Franklin to Cadwallader Colden, 1747 August 6, Mss.B.F85. Courtesy of the American Philosophical Society.

or asked Hays for guidance when more than one solution to a treatment problem presented itself. He also returned the books' detached covers. Berwick does not appear to have used before- and after-treatment photography except for public-relations purposes, and he did not provide the detailed written reports that today's conservation ethics require, so the specific materials and techniques he employed cannot always be determined. His letters and the treated documents, however, reveal a conscientious, highly skilled practitioner who took great pains to preserve historic texts without damage to ink or paper.

Indeed, Berwick's mastery of using silk gauze or crepeline to line and protect manuscripts appears to have been unequaled in the United States. In her book, Smith describes the evolution of fine silk as a conservation material, concluding that it likely developed from the adhesive-coated silk netting known as court plaster, which was used both cosmetically and medically in the eighteenth and nineteenth centuries. Carlo Marrè, a restorer employed by the Vatican Library, perfected the use of silk crepeline to reinforce the manuscripts there, and his methods were publicized by Prefect Franz Ehrle in an 1898 article and conference on manuscripts and iron gall ink. Herbert Friedenwald, then superintendent of the Department of Manuscripts at the Library of Congress, wrote to Ehrle while establishing the library's first restoration program and apparently introduced the Vatican method of silking to his employees. On October 27, 1900, Berwick wrote to Hays:

> Crepeline is wonderful stuff for this work & the more I use of it the better I like it. It seems to me that Dr. H. Freidenwald [sic] (whose resignation I very much regret) should be given due credit for his unremitting search for the best material to repair mss. & was, I believe, the first to introduce it into this country & for which all lovers of ancient mss should be grateful.

Today, Berwick's silked documents at the APS remain flat, strong, undarkened, and highly legible (see fig. 7). The paper handling margins and fills, which he shaped and beveled to fit each ragged edge or loss, continue to protect the original documents from harm while making each manuscript an aesthetic whole. Although the manuscripts were again disbound, unmounted, and placed into folders during the twentieth century, they often retain their tracing-cloth hinges. Berwick's repairs continue to allow the documents to be read and handled by APS researchers more than 100 years after they were made.

1935–1939: Carol Rugh (later Carolyn Horton), Book and Paper Conservator

Following Berwick's unexpected death in 1920, APS Librarian I. Minis Hays made inquiries about hiring another paper restorer, but it is unclear whether he found anyone right away. In 1935, Hays' successor Laura E. Hanson

(1871–1948), the Society's first professional librarian, hired its first in-house, part-time conservator, Carol Price Rugh (1909–2001), who became Carolyn Horton upon her remarriage.[18] According to a colleague's overview of Horton's career and accomplishments, she studied bookbinding at the Women's Academy of Applied Art in Vienna from 1929 to 1930, then apprenticed with German binder and restorer Albert Oldach in Philadelphia for five years.[19] At the APS, archival records show that she was paid $1 to $1.50 per hour to mend documents and repair books. With additional income from private binding and conservation work, Rugh was able to support herself and her sister through the Great Depression. When she left the APS Library in 1939, Rugh remarried. As Carolyn Horton, she went on to become the first book conservator at Yale University, then a binder and conservator in private practice and an expert responder after the Florence Flood in 1966. She is now recognized as a pioneer of modern book and paper conservation. Although her later name is famous within the conservation community, her earlier name will be used in this book when referencing work performed at the APS.

With Hanson's guidance, Rugh treated both manuscripts and printed materials, loose documents and bound volumes. To date, I have only been able to review Rugh's treatment records from 1935, which she evidently shared with the APS Library Committee in a report in October of that year. Willman Spawn later made a copy of her records (now held at Columbia University) to deposit in the APS Archives. In her report, Rugh notes, "As each piece of work was begun the value and probable use of the book was discussed with the librarian. The most elaborate restoring has been done only on priceless items."[20]

Although Rugh's work began in May 1935 with treatment of specific treasures from the Library's collection—including APS archival documents,

---

[18] Laura E. Hanson is listed among the 1897 graduates of Drexel Institute Library School in "Library Schools and Training Classes," *Library Journal* 22, no. 7 (1897): 358. She remains the only female APS Librarian in the Society's history, as well as the first of only two APS Librarians to have been trained as a librarian or archivist.

[19] Unless otherwise specified, details about Carolyn Horton's professional career in this paragraph are from Betsy Palmer Eldridge, "Carolyn Price Horton: 1909–2001," *Abbey Newsletter* 25, no. 5 (2002).

[20] Carol P. Rugh, "Record of work done for the American Philosophical Society by Carol Rugh, May 6, 1935 to December 31, 1935," 81. Unpublished conservation notes, American Philosophical Society Archives. Unless otherwise stated, all references to Rugh's treatment work are derived from these records.

copies of early American almanacs, and recently acquired letters from Benjamin Franklin—by July she had embarked on a survey of the Society's special collections to establish condition problems and treatment needs throughout the Library, an approach more aligned with preventive conservation. Her survey included the Mason Collection (likely a book donation from collector William Smith Mason) and the book collections in the Library's new fireproof rare-book and manuscript vaults. Her resulting notes for the Library Committee broke down needed repairs into manuscript mending (simple and complex), books that needed rebacking or re-gluing and re-casing (a method of repairing nineteenth-century bindings), books that needed resewing and/or rebinding, and books whose vellum covers required special attention. She also distinguished detached or broken leather bindings from cloth or paper bindings in similar condition.

Rugh's time with the Society corresponded with two crucial advances in the library conservation sphere. In the 1920s, Swedish chemists identified acidity or low pH as an important factor in the deterioration of paper.[21] Although sulfuric acid would not be identified as the culprit in accelerated leather decay until 1948, preservation specialists in libraries and museums were already aware that vegetable-tanned leathers produced since the Industrial Revolution were quick to deteriorate, and they sought both methods to slow this decay and alternative materials for repairing damaged leather. In England, Harold J. Plenderleith of the British Museum created a system for cleaning and dressing leather bindings in an attempt to slow their rapid deterioration, publishing his laboratory notes in the *British Museum Quarterly* and elsewhere beginning in 1927.[22]

Rugh was apparently aware of both of these developments, and she introduced the use of acid-free enclosures and the application of leather dressing during her tenure at the APS. In June 1935, Rugh's treatment notes refer to 1,818 books that were "washed, oiled & polished according to the British Museum formula & technique" and 568 labels that were "oiled and polished" (11). She evidently considered leather dressing part of routine maintenance, as she wrote to the APS Committee on the Library in May 1941 (when her offer was rejected) and in February 1942, offering to

---

[21] S. Kohler and G. Hall, "Acidity in Paper," *Paper Industry* 7, no. 7 (1925): 1059.

[22] Harold J. Plenderleith, "Laboratory Notes: The Preservation of Bookbindings," *British Museum Quarterly* 2, no. 3 (1927): 77–78.

oil the bindings again for six cents per volume.[23] Although leather dressing has since fallen out of favor with many conservators due to its potential side effects,[24] the use of acid-free or alkaline storage materials remains a primary strategy for the long-term protection of paper-based collections. Rugh's engagement with the latest developments in leather preservation and paper chemistry indicate her dedication to the preservation field and her willingness to alter traditional restoration techniques to accommodate new principles.

Two of Rugh's repair materials—Asian papers and chrome-tanned leather—also testify to her inventiveness and experimentation. Although Rugh relied on many of the materials Berwick had used—including silk crepeline (which she called chiffon), tracing cloth, and carefully selected Western papers—she also adopted new materials and methods for her more extensive book conservation treatments. Vegetable-tanned leathers— which rely on plant-based tanning agents such as sumac or oak bark—were traditionally used for bookbinding because they are easy to thin and pare and readily accept the impressions of heated decorative tools. Changes in air quality and tanning procedures after the Industrial Revolution, however, made vegetable-tanned leathers far more susceptible to rapid decay and far less useful as a repair material. Rugh's 1935 treatment notes for specific books (designated by their call numbers and often a short title) indicate that she rebacked decayed leather bindings with buckram (a coarse fabric stiffened and made impermeable with adhesive) or "new American chrome tanned calf" (71). Neither buckram nor chrome-tanned leather (both invented in the early nineteenth century) were widely used in the restoration of leather bindings at this date, and Rugh's use of leather tanned with chromium salts is particularly surprising. Chrome-tanned leather is the tough, flexible, rot-resistant leather used in modern car upholstery. It can be distinguished from other leathers by its distinctive blue-gray interior, even when its surface has been dyed another color. Although it is

---

[23] See the Committee on the Library Minutes for May 21, 1941, and February 12, 1942, American Philosophical Society Archives.

[24] Although conventional wisdom long encouraged the regular "feeding" of leather with oils and waxes, conservators now discourage the practice. Over time, the added fats and oils replace the water that keeps leather supple, and the leather becomes brittle and desiccated. Fats may also bloom to the surface of the leather, leaving a mottled waxy coating known as "spue." For an early article criticizing the unthinking use of leather dressings, see Toby Raphael and Ellen McCrady, "Leather Dressing: To Dress or Not To Dress," *Leather Conservation News* 1, no. 2 (1983): 9–10.

extremely durable, it is devilishly difficult to pare and tool.[25] Rugh's use of it illustrates both her determination and her commitment to the long-term preservation of the Society's collections.

Rugh's treatment notes also indicate that she frequently used Asian papers in her treatment work, although their use in restoration was not widespread in the 1930s. Long-fibered Korean papers (*hanji*) and Japanese papers (*washi*) made from the paper mulberry shrub are now a staple of book and paper conservation because they are strong, flexible, chemically stable, and offer a range of translucencies. The finest, thinnest papers are almost invisible when used as mending tissue. Rugh used Korean paper for guarding (mending the split spine folds of paper folios), hinging (attaching one sheet of paper to another), and mending. She often specified the use of "Japan vellum"—which may have been a thick, translucent Japanese paper or a Western paper made to imitate it—for guarding and strip-mending the edges of leaves.

In addition to her prescient use of Asian papers, Rugh employed a variety of time-honored and novel treatment methods and documented them for posterity. She soaked the original paper and leather coverings off damaged or rotten book boards and applied them to new boards. Rather than relying on uncertain supplies of antique Western paper, she often used modern Arches paper, both to make new pamphlet covers and to create false margins, which she tinted to match the hue of the original paper. Although most of this information is gleaned from the treatment notebook she kept for reporting to the Library Committee, the abbreviated treatment records she pasted into the backs of books are also pithy but informative (see fig. 8).

Like modern conservators, Rugh often addressed the problem of oversize maps folded into books. Such maps frequently tear along their hinges, split along their folds, or become misfolded after repeated use, resulting in soiling and damage where the map protrudes from the bookbinding. In Rugh's 1935 treatment of a 1613 German edition of Johann Theodor de Bry's *Small Voyages* with a modern binding, she removed all of the maps, cut them along their folds, and mounted them on cloth (other treatment notes specify "muslin") to prevent wear of the paper at the folds. Three of the maps were then re-sewn into the book, and the book

---

[25] For a book conservator's more recent experiments with the use of chrome-tanned leather, see Ann Lindsey, "Conservation Experience in Working with Chrome Tanned Leather," *Book and Paper Group Annual* 21 (2002): 99–103.

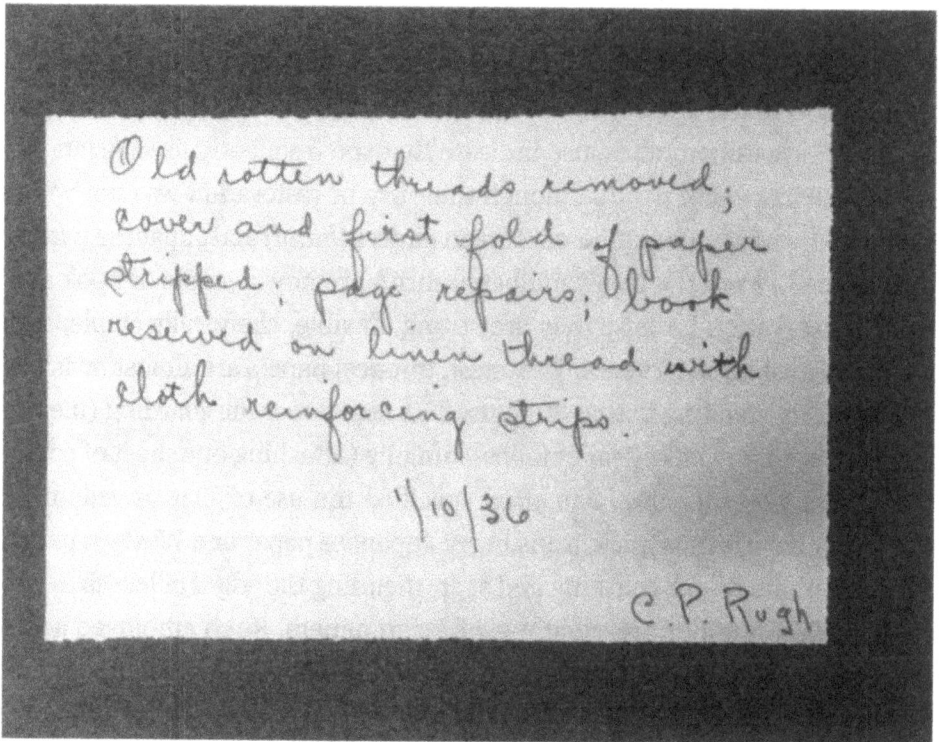

Old rotten threads removed; cover and first fold of paper stripped; page repairs; book resewed on linen thread with cloth reinforcing strips.

1/10/36

C. P. Rugh

Figure 8.   Carol Rugh's treatment slip for William Poyntell's 1803 thermometrical journal, a pamphlet stitched into a folio of marbled paper. In this case, Rugh pasted her treatment slip into the wrapper she created for the journal. Mss.551.5.P86, American Philosophical Society. Courtesy of the author.

was provided with a new binding. The last map in the book, which served as a general reference for the whole work, was provided with its own case of black library buckram. Similar treatment problems continue to vex today's library conservators. Although preserving a map in its original format is ideal, brittle paper or frequent use may make interventions like Rugh's necessary. Where a removed map requires a lining, today's conservators are more likely to employ a sturdy Asian paper than cotton or linen fabric. Librarians and conservators must work together to preserve the connection between the bound volume that once contained the map—often shelved with other books—and the map itself, which may be stored flat in a drawer elsewhere in the library.

Rugh's notes indicate that she also treated damaged wax seals, a conservation challenge unique to manuscript collections. In a summary detailing her restoration work from November 1, 1936, to April 30, 1937, she noted that "140 seals were pieced together and restored. Moulds of 34 of these were taken and are being cast in wax."[26] One hopes that further research may determine which seals have been recreated and how the pieced-together seals were restored.

In many ways, Rugh had a modern conservator's sense of what was right: She provided thoughtful estimates, documented her work, and used the best materials available to her. Her October 1935 report to the Library Committee listed the materials she was likely to need for the work covered in her condition survey, budgeting $100 for leather, "buckram, end papers, Japan vellum, repair paper, blotting paper, wax paper, glue, vellum, etc." and $80 for chiffon, "if no rebacking is to be done" (79). She valued her first 5.5 months of labor at $550 and her materials at $89.71 (equivalent to $10,350 and $1,690 in 2020). In explaining these costs, she wrote:

> Since labor is always by far the greatest expense in all such work, the entire effort has been to make the work as lasting as possible. A special effort has been made to use only the very best materials available, so that the work will not have to be done over in the years to come. All paper used has been imported hand-made all rag paper. Glue and paste have been of the best quality. All chemicals have been of U.S.P. [United States Pharmacopeia] quality.
>
> In restoring, the aim has been honest workmanship with no attempt to conceal the fact that work has been done. (81)

1942–1949: Helen A. Price, Book Conservator

After Rugh's departure for Yale in 1939 and Hanson's retirement in 1941, the October 21, 1942, Committee on the Library Minutes address the desire for a new book restorer:

> The assistant librarian spoke of the need for the repair of old books which it is thought inadvisable to send to a commercial binder, and said that it is possible to secure the services of Mrs. Helen A. Price to do this work in our own building at the rate of $1.00 an hour, plus the cost of materials. Dr. Moore recommended Mrs. Price and said that she had done some work of a similar nature for the Academy of Natural Sciences. The Committee agreed that the work should be done, and voted an appropriation of $500 with which to start.[27]

---

[26] [Carol] Rugh, "Summary of 6 Months Restoration Work at the American Philosophical Society, November 1, 1936–April 30, 1937." American Philosophical Society Archives.

[27] Committee on the Library Minutes, October 21, 1942, 5. American Philosophical Society Archives.

This note is valuable both for its reference to the use of commercial binders and for its recognition that not all books should receive commercial or library bindings. The distinguishing factors for the books thought to need special treatment remain tantalizingly vague, given the preponderance of rebound early books and manuscripts in the Society's collections (see page 18).

Following Price's mention in the Committee on the Library Minutes, she was evidently hired part-time by new APS Librarian William E. Linglebach (1871–1962), a historian who led the APS Library until 1958. Price's typed or handwritten slips may be found on treated books scattered throughout the Library's collection. According to her successor, Willman Spawn, Price also worked as restorer for the Philadelphia Register of Wills and left him a supply of silk chiffon (badly gnawed by cockroaches) for conservation work. Little more is now known about Price's training or previous experience, or about the specifics of her in-house treatments for the APS.

1948–1985: Willman Spawn, Book Conservator and Binding Historian

Willman Spawn (1920–2010), who studied bookbinding in the Works Progress Administration bindery at the Smithsonian as a teenager and later trained with Berwick protégé Augusta Hitchcock at the Massachusetts Historical Society, became the Society's third part-time conservator in 1948. He was hired at 10 hours per week, but he was promoted to full-time conservator in 1960, after the completion of Library Hall (see fig. 9). His groundbreaking contributions to the field of conservation lay in discoveries related to early American bindings, the development of strategies for responding to floods and leaks in libraries and archives, and the invention of new enclosures.

In a 2004 oral history interview, Spawn told Julie Baker:

> The work that the APS had me do initially was basically silking of manuscripts and repair[ing of] manuscripts in the collection. It wasn't until after I came [full time?] that we did any binding work, and after that it was mainly repair on some of the rare books, some of the books from Franklin's library and such. . . .
>
> I would say the first year I worked on nothing but Franklin items, and one or two Jefferson things. Later on, we got into some of the large maps and things that needed to be conserved. (2, 3)

Figure 9. Willman Spawn working in the Library Hall conservation lab in an undated photograph. APS Archives, graphics:9621. Courtesy of the American Philosophical Society.

During Spawn's career at the APS, he apparently kept treatment notes in a variety of ways. Even though I have not found any photographic documentation dating to Spawn's era, the APS Archives retain one of his treatment notebooks from 1948 to 1950 and a series of annotated typewritten work orders from 1960 to 1965. Given his concern with retaining the records of the conservators who went before him—including William Berwick and Carol Rugh—it seems likely that he kept additional treatment records, which may be located with his research papers. Books that Spawn is said to have bound or rebacked—he did not attach slips summarizing his treatment as Rugh and Price had done—reveal that he continued on the path his predecessors had established. He silked manuscripts using rice starch paste, applied guards of bond paper, rebacked in leather, and provided new cloth or paper case bindings to replace earlier bindings that no longer served to protect their contents. His oral history reveals that he also split manuscripts through their thickness and adhered a new paper core between the separated layers to strengthen them.

Spawn's relatively conservative approach to conservation treatment was likely a boon to the Society's collections. His long tenure with the APS roughly overlapped with the popularity of self-taught chemist and paper restorer William Barrow (1904–1967), who used new information about paper chemistry—including a Canadian patent for neutralizing paper pulp at the mill using alkaline earth metals[28]—to develop and market his own methods for deacidifying and laminating paper. In his private paper restoration studio, Barrow washed documents in water or solvents containing magnesium salts to alkalize the paper and prevent acid-based deterioration. Although calcium salts have since replaced magnesium in washing solutions, alkalization of historic papers is still a common practice and can drastically prolong the useful life of documents. Barrow, however, went one step further. He sandwiched deacidified documents between sheets of transparent paper and cellulose acetate, the plastic used in safety film, and laminated them together using high heat and pressure. Only after millions of documents had been preserved in this way did conservators discover that the cellulose acetate emits acetic acid as it ages. The resulting acidic environment can actually speed the deterioration of the laminated documents, and the plastic can only be removed by hand, with the aid of large amounts of toxic solvents.[29] Despite this setback, Barrow remained influential with institutional clients worldwide, including the Library of Congress, the Virginia State Library, and archives in Europe. Fortunately, the APS was not among them. Neither Spawn nor his successors experimented with cellulose acetate lamination, which was extremely popular from the 1930s to the 1980s.

The Report of the Committee on Library for 1964 provides some insight into the Society's preservation activities during Spawn's tenure. Over the course of the year, "in order to facilitate future use of the collections, some 1,200 volumes were bound, 140 rare books were restored, and 126 slipcases

---

[28] "Deacidification at the Mill: An Early Patent," *Alkaline Paper Advocate* 2, no. 2 (July 1989).

[29] For more information about cellulose acetate lamination and the challenges it poses to conservators and collectors, see Eddie Woodward, "The Epidemic in the Archives: A Layman's Guide to Cellulose Acetate Lamination," *RBM: A Journal of Rare Books, Manuscripts, and Cultural Heritage* 18, no. 2 (2017).

were made for rare books and pamphlets."[30] In his oral history, Spawn expressed frustration that books continued to be sent out for binding (either to commercial binders or trained artisans like Fritz and Trudi Eberhardt) without his input. Yet Spawn seems to have been held in high esteem within the organization, perhaps because of his demand as a teacher within the wider conservation community and because of his own academic prowess. The same report also states:

> Mr. Spawn, Restorer of Manuscripts, spent several weeks during the Spring in giving instruction to trainees at the Toronto Public Library and the University of Toronto. During the summer, aided by a grant from the Society's Penrose Fund, he was on leave in order to continue research on eighteenth-century American bookbinders. He worked primarily at Boston, Worcester, Providence, and Newport. At the Newport Historical Society he arranged an exhibit and spoke on Francis Skinner, 1708–1785, a binder in that city for more than fifty years. (187)

As the report suggests, Spawn became a recognized authority on early American binders through studying their tool marks in extant leather bindings. The impressions of hand stamps or rolls on bindings known to be produced by specific individuals—such as Robert Aitken or Francis Skinner—allowed Spawn to attribute previously anonymous bindings with the same tool marks to their historical binders. He urged other conservators and restorers to retain original bindings whenever possible, so their historical evidence would not be lost, and the reuse and retention of existing binding material is now a critical tenet of book conservation.

Many libraries across the country—including Case Western Reserve Library, Temple University Law Library, the Wilmington Public Library, and the Free Library of Philadelphia—also benefited from Spawn's expertise and generosity in responding to leaks and other water disasters. In his oral history, he described sandwiching wet documents between waxed paper and felts so they would dry rapidly without developing mold. When time was of the essence, he experimented with refrigerating and vacuum freeze-drying wet library collections, a response that has since become a disaster-response standard.

---

[30] "Report of the Committee on Library for 1964," *Proceedings of the American Philosophical Society* 109 (1965): 189.

Spawn also taught staff at local institutions to make "the Spawn wrapper" or "Spawn box," a book housing he invented to prepare the APS Library for its many moves. The wrapper is quick to make and requires no adhesive, but its operation can be mysterious to the uninitiated. It is now found in many library collections throughout the Delaware Valley. According to Spawn's oral history, he (like Rugh) was concerned about acid migration and continued to advocate for the use of pH-neutral housings and book boards at the APS. Shortly before his retirement in 1985, Spawn feverishly built thousands of his wrappers to protect the Library's non-rare printed books during their move to Franklin Hall.

After his retirement, Spawn served as Honorary Curator of Book-bindings at Bryn Mawr College and continued his research on bindings until his death in 2010. Bryn Mawr has since donated his papers to the Society, where they currently await processing. One hopes that their contents may eventually contribute further details about eighteenth-century bindings and mid-century conservation practices to the literature on those subjects.

1960s–1970s: Fritz and Trudi Eberhardt, Bookbinders and Restorers

Although Willman Spawn preferred to retain original bindings, he could not do all of the book repair required by a growing special collections library. As it had in the past, the APS continued to send many of its damaged books out for repair and rebinding through the late twentieth century. In 1965, the APS Committee on Library discussed sending the books in Franklin's library to Harold W. Tribolet of R. R. Donnelley and Sons, Chicago, or to Joseph Ruzicka of Baltimore.[31] It is unclear whether the Committee's recommendations were pursued, but many rare books were certainly sent out for repair and returned without their original bindings. Hedi Kyle's 1993 review of conservation practices at the Society lists surviving commercial binding records for "MacDonald in New York, Storm in Arizona, and Wessely in England" and notes that "the practice of sending serials out

---

[31] Committee on the Library, 1965. Unprocessed Executive Committee files, American Philosophical Society Archives.

to library binderies continues and results in approximately 400 hardbound volumes per year."[32]

In the 1960s and 1970s, two of the Society's contract binders were Fritz Eberhardt (1917–1997) and Trudi Eberhardt (1921–2004). The couple apprenticed as bookbinders in their native Germany, and Fritz also attended the Academy for Graphic Arts in Leipzig and the Offenbach School of Fine Arts for binding and calligraphy, becoming a master binder. After World War II, Fritz escaped Soviet Eastern Europe on foot, despite a leg that had been lamed by childhood polio. He later met Trudi, and the two married in Sweden, eventually emigrating to Philadelphia in 1954. Their characteristic leather bindings—with rounded spines, crisp raised bands, gold-tooled titles, and flattened endcaps—can be found at the APS and in many other local institutions.

These bindings offended Spawn's sensibilities when applied to early American books, but he apparently had no say in whether or which rare books were sent out for repair. In his oral history, he complained (likely of Fritz Eberhardt),

> that he had restored a book in a good Scottish binding of Robert Aitken's that had been perfectly [planned] and efficiently done in 1779 in Philadelphia by Robert Aitken, and it looked like a German binding with gold tooling. It was so inappropriate that it really bothered me, and it made me realize that any binding that I saw in the APS collection, that the only way I could protect it was to make a very nice box for it and keep it out of sight. Because if the book was preserved in a box, it wouldn't be sent out for restoration. I am grateful for the books that I saved in the collection by putting [them] in a case. (9–10)

Although the Eberhardts are primarily remembered as contract binders, they evidently performed a fair amount of book restoration as well. In a 1993 oral history, Fritz recalled their early days in Philadelphia, repairing and binding pamphlets for Edwin Wolf II (1911–1991), Library Company Librarian:

> We had—our workload doing pamphlets, the rebinding, maltreated and raped pamphlets, abused pamphlets [that we put] into their own

---

[32] Hedi Kyle, "Conservation at the American Philosophical Society: An Institutional Profile in 1992," in *The Changing Role of Book Repair in ARL Libraries* (Washington, DC: Association of Research Libraries, 1993), 1.

little hard cover with a title on. Washing them, cleaning them, mending them and all that. And they went, at the beginning, for $3.00 a piece, finished. . . . We took them in lots of one hundred.[33]

In the same interview, Trudi reported, "There was a lot of paper repair in the beginning. That's very technical work" (52). The Eberhardts had not been trained in restoration when they emigrated, but they found that American clients were far more willing to pay a living wage for the restoration of historical documents than for well-made new bindings. Trudi stated:

> We, of course, both learned bookbinding and not restoration because that wasn't done at that time. And when we came to this country, there was more and more need for it. For restoration. And so a lot of things we figured out for ourselves but then we figured out we should go back to Germany sometime and see what they're doing. Because . . . [after] the World War, there were lots of libraries who needed restoration. (73)

In 1972 the couple returned to Munich, Göttingen, and Wolfenbüttal and, according to Trudi, "visited several different institutions that had restoration workshops. And they were very accommodating. They showed us everything we wanted to see and we learned . . . quite a lot there" (73).

By the time the Eberhardts studied restoration in Germany, they had been living and working in rural Harleysville, Pennsylvania, for a decade. The majority of the Eberhardts' work for the Society likely occurred during this period, while medical historian Richard Shryock and Franklin historian Whitfield Bell, Jr. (1914–2009) served as APS Librarians. As Trudi said:

> At the time, we mostly worked for the rare book collection of universities. And they didn't just come from around here. We worked for Wyoming, for the University of Connecticut, then Arizona for a while, Rice University. And so on and so forth. They came from all over. So it was very good that we could just stay at home, do the work, pack it up, and send it out. (81)

The Eberhardts also trained binders who were serious about learning traditional hand skills, including Don Rash, who studied with them for several

---

[33] Fritz Eberhardt and Trudi Eberhardt, "An oral history of Fritz and Trudi Eberhardt, conducted by Valerie A. Metzler, Archivist/Historian, on 6 and 7 July, 1993, at the Eberhardt home outside Schwenksville, Pennsylvania," *Guild of Bookworkers Journal* 37, no. 2 (2002): 51. Unless otherwise stated, all references to the Eberhardts are drawn from this oral history.

Figure 10. Hedi Kyle assists a student with a folded paper structure in an undated photograph. APS Archives, graphics:9785. Courtesy of the American Philosophical Society.

years. Rash later taught me to bind books following the Eberhardt model, although I was his student for months rather than years. Thus, in a roundabout way, the Eberhardts' work continues to influence the collections at the APS. Further research in the APS Archives may reveal the extent of their original contributions to the Society's Library.

1986–2003: Hedi Kyle, Book Artist and Conservator

Hedi Kyle (b. 1937) became head of conservation at the APS after Willman Spawn's retirement (see fig. 10). Like the Eberhardts, she had trained as an artist in Germany before emigrating to the United States in the early 1960s. In the 1970s, she studied with bookbinder and early book conservator Laura Young (1905–1996) in New York, and from 1979 to 1985 she served as head conservator at the New York Botanical Garden. Shortly after she was hired at the APS in 1986, she renovated and enlarged the conservation lab in Library Hall. She also created the first APS Library disaster plan with book conservator Gail Harriman.

Kyle's 1993 overview of conservation changes at the APS suggests that the lion's share of her work involved rehousing the collections, and she often taught workshops on the construction of boxes, wrappers, and folders. The book housings produced by Kyle and her trainees were always thoughtfully constructed and sometimes gorgeously decorated, incorporating bright bookcloth, paste papers, or dyed Tyvek. In addition to rehousing books, Kyle and her assistants performed full treatments on flat paper and bound documents, including aqueous washing and sun-bleaching. For two decades, Kyle also mentored graduate book arts students at the University of the Arts, many of whom—notably Denise Carbone (b. 1957), who became APS book conservator after Kyle's retirement—later served as interns or staff in the APS conservation lab. Kyle's most enduring legacies since her retirement in 2003 have been as a book artist and teacher. Her iconic book designs continue to draw inspiration from historic bindings and her conservation experience.

Kyle and her staff certainly kept records of their work during treatment, because they routinely reported the total number of items and pages treated to the APS Library Committee. These reports rarely include the details of what treatment involved, however, and the surviving documentation is scarce. The conservators and interns may have retained their own records rather than placing them in a physical or digital archive at the Library, although some handwritten and digital records have been found. Rough treatment notes occasionally accompany partially treated materials, and they range from interns' handwritten notes and diagrams to a variety of preprinted condition and treatment forms. The detailed book-treatment form used in the 2000s provided spaces for recording binding and sewing structures, condition problems, and repair methods and materials. Full written and photographic documentation does not appear to have been the norm for even the most complex book treatments, and final treatment reports were not routinely included with repaired library books. Those that have been found range from full printed reports with photographs to handwritten slips. It is hoped that further research in the APS Archives will uncover more information about the book treatments undertaken during this period.

Conservation at the APS Library & Museum Today

When this book was written, the APS employed three conservators with master's degrees in art conservation: Anne Downey, Anisha Gupta, and myself. Downey, Head of Conservation, has a degree in paper conservation from SUNY Buffalo State, where she studied the chemistry, construction, and repair of prints, drawings, pastels, and watercolors as well as archival documents and manuscripts. Before joining the APS in 2003, Downey worked as a paper conservator at the Conservation Center for Art and Historic Artifacts (CCAHA), a regional conservation center in Philadelphia. Assistant Conservator Anisha Gupta discovered art conservation while she was still in high school, during an advanced-placement class in art history. Gupta went on to complete a double major in chemistry and art history at the University of Illinois Urbana-Champaign. She has a master's degree in paper conservation with a minor in photograph conservation from the Winterthur/University of Delaware Program in Art Conservation. Prior to joining the APS in 2018, Gupta worked at the Fine Arts Museums of San Francisco, the Cleveland Museum of Art, the Tate, and the University of Illinois Library.[34] After a first career as a writer and editor, I studied book and paper conservation at the Winterthur/University of Delaware Program in Art Conservation. Before joining the APS, where I am now Assistant Head of Conservation and Book Conservator, I worked at the National Portrait Gallery, the New York Public Library, the Walters Art Museum, and CCAHA, where I was promoted to book conservator. I also taught book history and book conservation in the undergraduate conservation program at the University of Delaware. Thanks to our graduate training and diverse experiences, my colleagues and I possess extensive knowledge of conservation ethics, materials science, chemical principles, and recent developments in library conservation, all of which we employ in the treatment work now performed at the APS.

Shortly after Downey joined the APS in 2003, she oversaw the design of a new, larger conservation laboratory in Franklin Hall, with bench space for four workers. Even though it has the disadvantage of being separated from the rare book and manuscript collections by a busy city street,

---

[34] In 2021, while this book was with the publisher, Gupta left the APS to pursue a doctorate in Preservation Studies at the University of Delaware.

it provides space for treatments that could not be accommodated within Library Hall. The laboratory contains a wet treatment area, a humidification cabinet, mobile drying racks, a fume hood, chemical storage, and a separate room for mold remediation and examination using ultraviolet light. In 2019, part of the space was revamped to include a tethered-capture digital photography system, which has made photographic documentation far more efficient.

Documentation is now far more standardized than ever before. All treatments are logged by call number, title, and date, with—at minimum— brief statements of initial condition and the treatment performed. Any treatments that go beyond minor, routine repairs also require full written and photographic documentation. Condition reports and before-treatment photographs describe an artifact's materials, how it was made, and its current condition, including both chemical and physical damage. Treatment proposals offer one or more options for how the damage might be repaired, and these are often discussed with the appropriate librarian or curator to select a course of action. Treatment reports and after-treatment photographs describe the methods and materials used for repair and explain why a given treatment approach was selected. New file-naming and organizational protocols ensure that today's treatment records will remain accessible to future conservators. Any hard-copy treatment records are scanned to PDF and retained. The contents of treatment records are also entered into Mimsy XG, a collections-management database that the Library shares with the Museum. Gradually, legacy conservation records will be entered as well.

Hands-on rehousing and repair of collections material remain a high priority for the APS Library & Museum, with forty to sixty percent of each conservator's time spent at the bench. Although conservators continue to create specialized enclosures for unusual library collections, their focus is now on item-level conservation treatment and preventive care. The Society orders most of its custom book boxes from one of the many vendors with programmable board-cutting machines. Two fantastic volunteers handle the measurement and housing of new accessions. Almost every year, the APS conservation lab also accepts either a conservation graduate student or a preprogram candidate into the paid Willman Spawn Conservation Internship, with a focus on treatment and overall collections care.

CHAPTER 3

Generations of Re-Treatment at the APS Library & Museum

Given the long history of the APS, it is not unusual for today's conservators to confront books, manuscripts, and other documents that have been treated before. Their need for treatment may stem from exhibition, researcher or staff use, or special significance to donors. The Library recently established an "adopt-a-book" program, for example, that has sponsored conservation treatment for several decrepit volumes, some with great historic value and some that are interesting purely for their structure. The two biggest drivers for re-treatment, however, are exhibition and regular use.

In 2019, the APS Library and APS Museum (one entity until their collections were separated in 2000) were reintegrated to form the APS Library & Museum. Even before reintegration, the Society served not only reading-room researchers but also the museum-going public, and the conservators' more interventive treatments have often stemmed from exhibition preparation. Until the 2020 pandemic disrupted normal operations, the APS Museum mounted an exhibition in Philosophical Hall each year, generally from April 15 to December 31. Although the Museum exhibitions typically include three-dimensional objects and paintings as well as printed books and archival documents, APS Library holdings predominate. At the start of each exhibition cycle, the conservators assess the physical and chemical stability of Library materials proposed for exhibition and treat them when necessary, even when that means undoing a previous conservator's work.

Use in the Library—whether by visiting researchers or APS staff—is another factor that drives conservation treatment of books and manuscripts. Items that require stabilization for safe handling range widely, from overstuffed scrapbooks assembled with pressure-sensitive tape to oversize folded maps. Some of the most frequently handled objects are the most iconic books and documents in the Library's possession, which see constant use on tours for donors and other Library visitors. In many cases, these "treasures" have received repeated conservation interventions over their long history with the Library. Treatment for the bound volumes among these treasures—books that once belonged to figures like Benjamin Franklin or Charles Willson Peale—often goes beyond stabilization and into restoration. Today's librarians often desire such books to look intact and "well cared for," leading to the repair of minor visible damage that does not affect the book's function. Informed discussion about the pros and cons of such an approach is a necessary part of establishing a treatment plan.

The following case studies describe treatments carried out in the last two decades on Library materials that had been treated at least once before. Their former restorers and conservators include William Berwick, Carol Rugh, Willman Spawn, and Denise Carbone. These men and women used the information, intelligence, skills, and materials at their disposal to prolong the utility of the APS collections. In some cases, their methods and materials did not age well, and their repairs were removed because they were causing physical or chemical damage. In other cases, former treatments introduced errors such as mispagination, or caused discoloration and staining in paper. In still others, the former repairs had nothing to do with the reasons for re-treatment, and their retention or removal was merely a byproduct of treatment designed to address a completely separate condition issue.

David Rittenhouse, Diaries, 1784–1785 and 1792–1805, Mss.B.R51d

In addition to serving as one of the earliest APS Librarians, David Rittenhouse (1732–1796) was a Philadelphia instrument-maker, astronomer, and surveyor, as well as treasurer of Pennsylvania and the first director of the U.S. Mint. A self-taught mathematical genius, Rittenhouse built clocks, orreries, and telescopes; observed the 1769 transit of Venus across the sun from his own private observatory; and assisted with the 1784–1785 survey extending the Mason-Dixon Line to the southwest corner of Pennsylvania.

The APS holds two of Rittenhouse's diaries. The first covers the period from 1784 to 1785, and it includes both meteorological observations and notes from his surveying trip in western Pennsylvania. The second contains

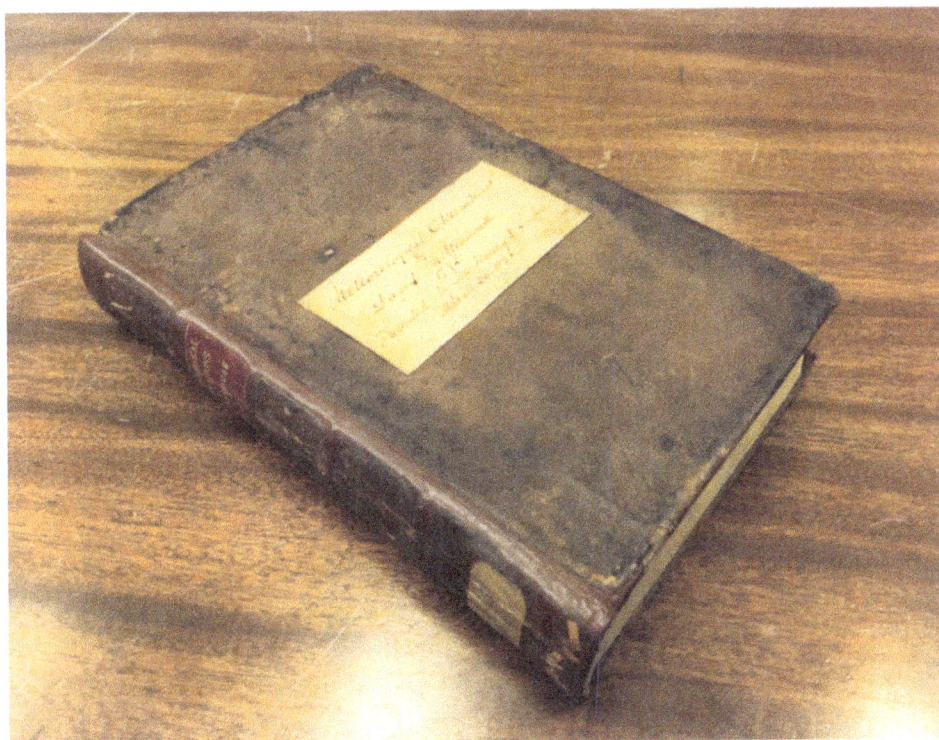

Figure 11. David Rittenhouse diary, 1792–1805, Mss.B.R51d vol. 2, American Philosophical Society. Carol Rugh rebacked this volume in chrome-tanned calf in 1936. Denise Carbone performed additional mending in 2007. Courtesy of the author.

meteorological observations from 1792 to 1805; these were carried on by family members for nine years after Rittenhouse's death. Recently, it was discovered that the two diaries display the work of three generations of book conservators at the APS. Both volumes were displayed open in the APS Museum's 2007 *Undaunted* exhibition, which seems to have been the catalyst for their most recent treatment.

The later and larger of the two books retains its original binding, but with substantial alterations (see fig. 11). Carol Rugh mended the leaves of the book in 1936. She also consolidated the leather (presumably using the British Museum's protocols), sewed new endbands at the top and bottom of the spine, and rebacked the book with chrome-tanned calf. In 2007, Denise Carbone treated the book again, mending additional edge tears, reinforcing the leather edges, and setting down the lifting front label. Both conservators documented their work with handwritten slips and minimal information about the materials used (see fig. 12).

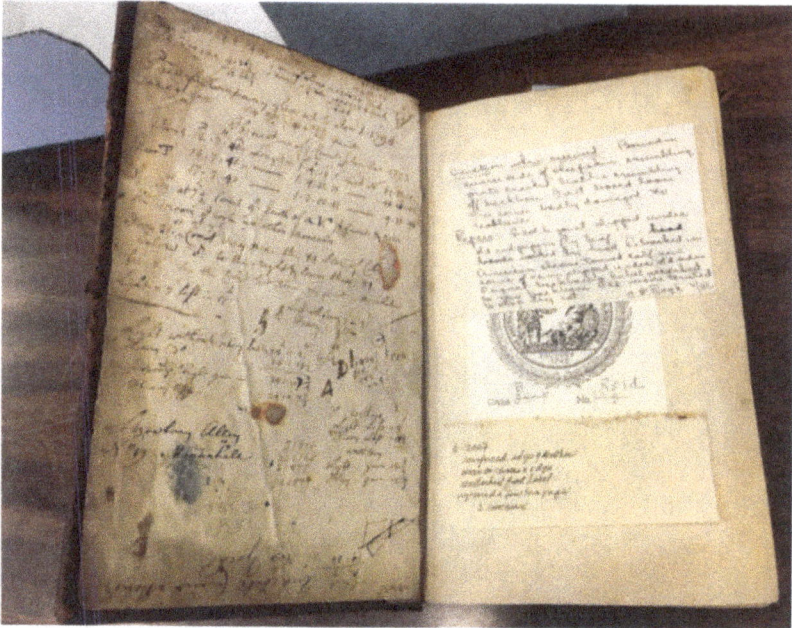

Figure 12. David Rittenhouse diary, 1792–1805, Mss.B.R51d vol. 2, American Philosophical Society. Carol Rugh's and Denise Carbone's pithy handwritten treatment slips (from July 1936 and June 2007, respectively) are adhered to the front flyleaf of the volume. Courtesy of the author.

The first diary underwent far more extensive alterations prior to exhibition, and it no longer resembles an eighteenth-century book. According to another of Carbone's handwritten slips, the diary's original leather binding was rebacked by Willman Spawn in the 1950s (see fig. 13), presumably because the leather spine had deteriorated. Carbone removed this rebacked binding in 2007, perhaps because it opened poorly. Condition notes from the museum's item list for *Undaunted* say that the binding was "bad," with leaves "cracking and falling out." Disbinding the book might have been necessary to make needed repairs to the text block and to allow the book to open far enough for display. After exhibition, however, the original binding was not reattached, as it almost certainly would be today. Instead, it was retained and provided with an interior support of corrugated alkaline paperboard. The note left with this support does not provide any context for the treatment beyond the date and Spawn's prior involvement with the binding (see fig. 14). Today, the rationale and procedures for a treatment of this scale are always included in the written conservation documentation,

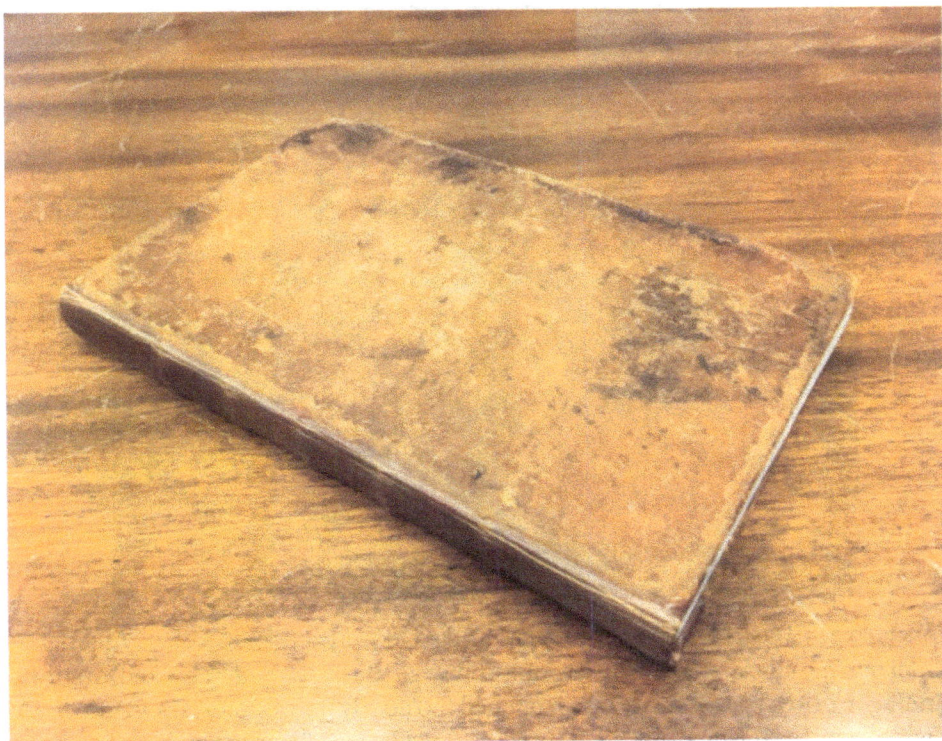

Figure 13.   David Rittenhouse diary, 1784–1785, Mss.B.R51d vol. 1, American Philosophical Society. Willman Spawn allegedly rebacked the original binding for this volume in the 1950s. Courtesy of the author.

as they provide crucial information for later conservators and researchers.

The first diary is now sewn into a contemporary variant of the medieval laced-case binding executed in heavy brown paper (see fig. 15). Case bindings have covers that are constructed separately from the text block, or the sewn-together leaves of the book. Modern trade bindings are cloth-covered cases attached to the outermost leaves of the text block with synthetic adhesive. In older case bindings, as in Carbone's contemporary version, the case was attached by lacing the ends of the book's sewing supports through slits in the joints of a parchment or heavy paper wrapper (the case), without the use of any adhesive. Non-adhesive paper bindings like these were frequently employed during Kyle's and Carbone's tenures at the Society, and they provide incontrovertible visual evidence that the object has been treated. They also generally open very flat, which would have been helpful during exhibition. Although I would likely pursue a different approach to treating this diary,

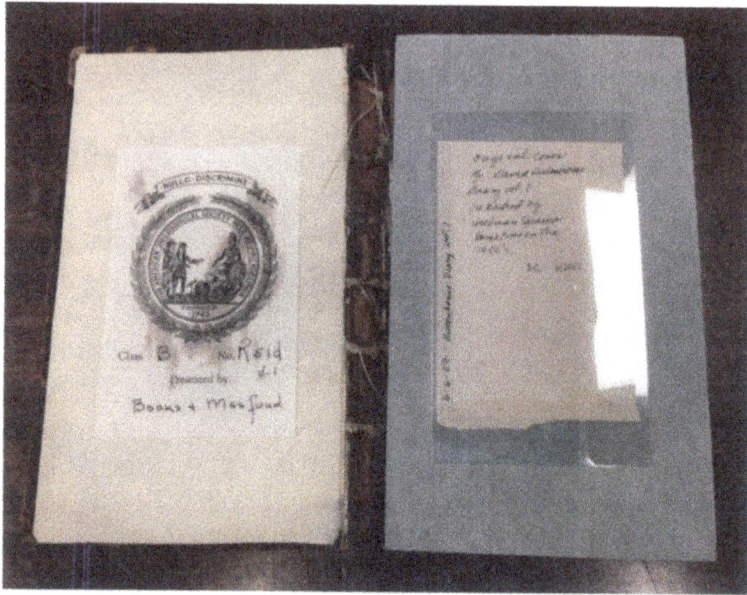

Figure 14. David Rittenhouse diary, 1784–1785, Mss.B.R51d vol. 1, American Philosophical Society. Denise Carbone removed the volume's rebacked original binding in 2007, probably because it opened too poorly for exhibition, and provided it with an internal support of alkaline corrugated board. Courtesy of the author.

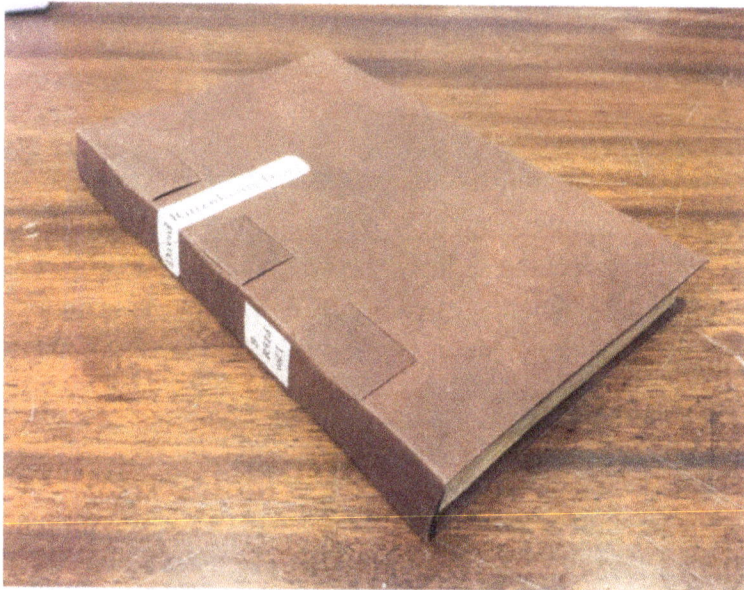

Figure 15. David Rittenhouse diary, 1784–1785, Mss.B.R51d vol. 1, American Philosophical Society. Denise Carbone rebound the volume in a contemporary paper variation of the laced-case structure. The unlined spine allows for unrestricted opening. Courtesy of the author.

reusing as much original material as possible, the laced-case binding is not causing harm and is not scheduled for replacement. The question may be revisited in the future if returning the book to its original context becomes a priority. Original or historic bindings can provide vital clues to a book's age, former importance, and use. Repairing and reusing them is now standard practice at the APS.

Vocabulary of the Delaware Indians, Mss.497.V85 no.17

Thomas Jefferson (1743–1826), who served as president of both the United States and the APS, was convinced that a comparative study of American Indigenous languages would reveal their common roots and suggest how recently each tribe had diverged from a common ancestral tongue. To support his theory, he collected lists of Native vocabulary words. Around 1791, he had large vocabulary forms printed with English words, and he asked friends and military officers across the young United States to fill in the forms with the words' Indigenous equivalents. Each large printed sheet contained about 280 English words on each side, beginning with "fire," "water," "air," and "earth," and moving on to days and seasons, the weather, body parts, types of people, and different birds and animals.

Jefferson had collected hundreds of these vocabulary sheets by the time he left office as president of the United States in 1809, and he had also created lists comparing the words from different languages to one another. He packed the one-of-a-kind manuscripts in a trunk for shipment to Monticello, but en route thieves mistook the trunk for a different sort of treasure and rifled its contents. Disappointed to find only documents, they flung the comparative vocabulary lists into the James River. The few surviving sheets, gathered by the APS Historical and Literary Committee in 1816 for publication, remained stained by mud and mold. Many of them were in tatters (see fig. 16). Given their historical importance and lamentable condition, APS Librarian I. Minis Hays shipped them to William Berwick for restoration in late 1913, after he had finished work on the Benjamin Franklin papers. Berwick also treated the few surviving printed vocabulary forms.

The printed vocabulary lists were quite large, roughly 19.5 × 13.5 inches, with identical printed matter on both sides of each sheet. Generally, only

Figure 16.   This fragment is from one of the many sheets on which Thomas Jefferson compared the Native words collected from his vocabulary forms. The comparative vocabularies suffered extremely when thieves threw them into the James River. According to his letter to I. Minis Hays on January 24, 1914, William Berwick split this fragment to avoid covering any of Jefferson's handwriting with fills. The split halves were then mounted on blank paper the size of the original document, provided with a frame, and silked. Thomas Jefferson, Comparative vocabularies of several Indian languages, 1802–1808, Mss.497.J35. Courtesy of the American Philosophical Society.

one side of each sheet was filled out, typically in iron gall ink, leaving a blank form on the other. Berwick treated three completed vocabulary forms for the Delaware, Miami, and Nanticoke tribes. Prior to his involvement, the sheets appear to have been folded vertically down the center and stitched through the fold. In 1913, however, the Society's intention seems to have been to bind the miscellaneous contents of the American Indian Vocabularies Collection (now Mss.497.V85) into one book, incorporating both the small and over-size manuscripts. Berwick addressed this challenge in his October 24, 1913, letter to Hays:

> I have examined the Miami & Delaware language sheets. It seems a pity to take them out of the rest of the collection & bind them on larger sheets. It would not do to mount them as in Dummy A inclosed—but would there be any objection to mounting them like Dummy B? The fold would be at the front instead of the back of the ledger paper but the reading matter would not be interfered with as in Dummy A in which the fold would break the reading matter in half on the back side.

Although the "dummies" Berwick refers to have disappeared, it can be inferred that both mockups featured a vocabulary list cut in half horizontally, with the two halves separated and mounted within a larger sheet of ledger paper. In each case, the mounted list was rotated 90 degrees and the central margin of ledger paper was folded to create a folio. In Dummy A, the fold (with the new-cut edges of the manuscript adjacent to it) was bound into the gutter or "back" of the book. In Dummy B, the fold was placed at the fore-edge of the book rather than in the gutter. Opening the fore-edge fold in option B would allow the list to be read in its entirety on both the front and the back, which would be impossible with option A.

Hays's feedback to Berwick's question is unknown, but Berwick apparently decided that even option B was too unwieldy for long-term preservation of the vocabulary lists. He worked on the vocabularies during his 1913 Christmas and New Year's holidays and shipped the completed documents to Hays by American Express on January 5, 1914. In his accompanying letter, Berwick wrote:

> The fault in doing the large vocabularies like the dummy I sent you was that to leave the writing intact it was necessary to hinge them at the end, & in turning over these large sheets the danger of tearing them would be great. The only way to avoid this & at the same time to make them handier to read was to split the paper, when of course the inner side of the (now) two sheets would be blank. This has been done. Each sheet was then lined & crepelined as usual....

Figure 17a. William Berwick's treatment portfolio, which his descendants donated to the American Philosophical Society in 2006, includes two samples of split music sheets. Here, the sheet has been split in preparation for further repair, and Berwick has signed one of the split sheets on its interior surface. Unprocessed William Berwick Family Collection. Courtesy of the American Philosophical Society.

> Splitting paper which can easily be replaced if spoiled is comparatively easy but with an old document only one of its kind & covered with writing is rather more hazardous, but I had no doubt of the result of the operation, although quite tedious.

Berwick did not reveal his technique for splitting the paper, but his treatment portfolio—which he kept for marketing rather than documentation purposes—includes several samples of split-paper documents (see figs. 17a and 17b). Examining the samples, which have not yet been processed, may reveal some of the details of his treatment methods. According to paper conservators Irene Brückle and Jana Dambrogio, paper splitting historically

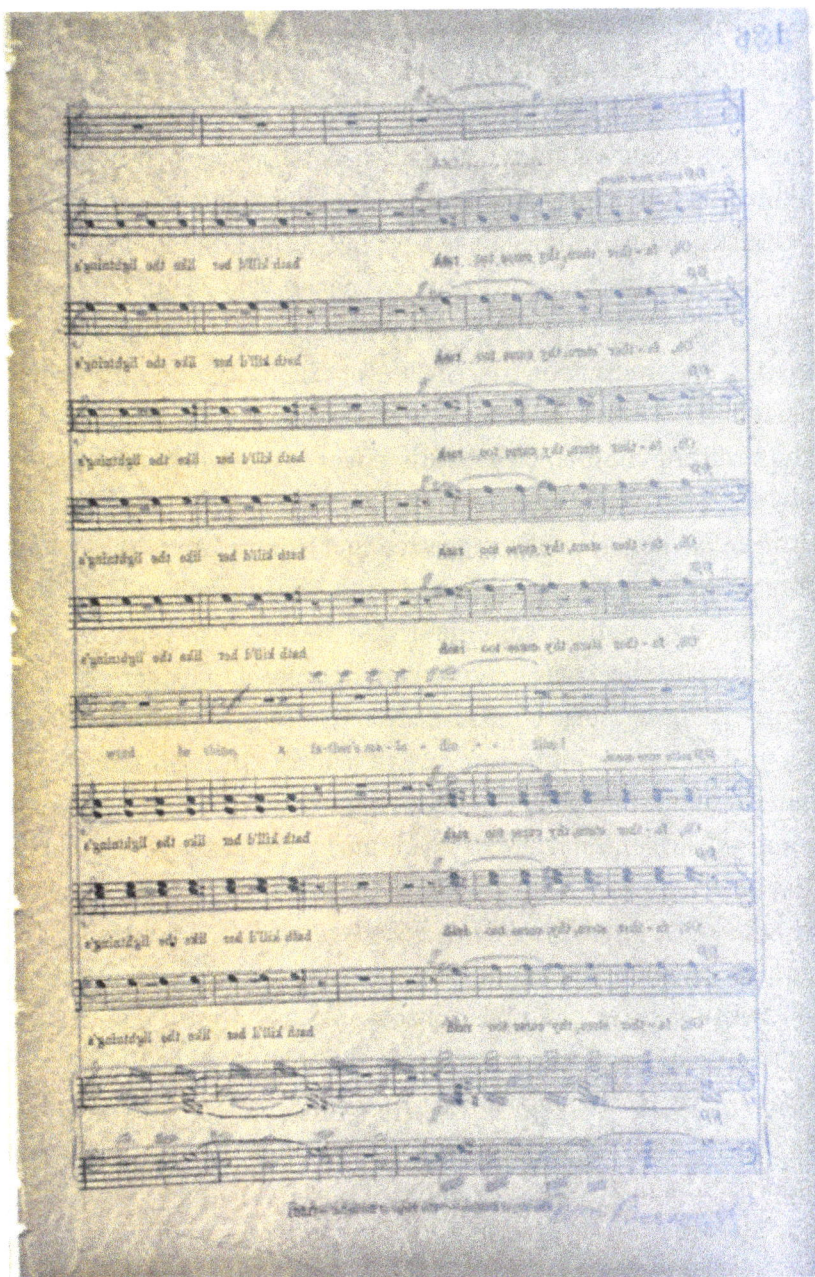

Figure 17b. Here, the halves of a similar sheet of music have been laminated to either side of a new paper core. Berwick's signature on the interior can be seen in transmitted light. Unprocessed William Berwick Family Collection. Courtesy of the American Philosophical Society.

involved facing both sides of the paper with a viscous adhesive and over-hanging support sheets, and then peeling the halves apart while the center of the paper remained damp. The separated halves might be lined separately, as in Berwick's treatment of the printed vocabulary sheets, or rejoined over a strengthening core paper (see fig. 16). Today, manual paper splitting often employs thick gelatin to attach the facing papers and a starch-based adhesive or cellulose derivative to secure any core paper. The facing papers can be removed with warm water, which will not dissolve the inner adhesive layer.[35]

Berwick apparently cut the sheets for the Delaware and Nanticoke Indians in half horizontally along a previous fold. He then split the halves, lined the resulting thinner sheets with ledger paper, and silked them. The two halves of each sheet were then provided with a cloth hinge for binding in the format he had originally suggested for "Dummy A," with the hinge in the gutter of the book (see figs. 18a and 18b). The blank form from the back of the Delaware vocabulary was mounted in the same way (fig. 19). The split Miami vocabulary sheet was mounted on four pieces of ledger paper rather than two, perhaps because it had already split along its central vertical fold. Berwick provided each of the four quarters of the sheet with an additional false margin of antique paper along its horizontal cut edge, apparently to match the leaf size of the rest of the volume more closely (see fig. 20). The mounted quarters were likely sewn into the book through hinges attached to their left edges, which have since been removed. It is not clear whether the blank backs of the Miami and Nanticoke vocabularies were retained.

None of this history had been discovered when the Delaware vocabulary form (see fig. 18a) was treated prior to display in the Society's 2006 *Treasures of the APS* exhibition. In her 2003 treatment report, Anne Downey noted that the form "had been restored within recent years," an ironic testament to the durability of Berwick's ninety-year-old restoration. She went on to describe how the form had been cut, mounted onto heavy wove paper, and laminated with silk, with a cloth hinge (likely Berwick's favorite tracing cloth) attached over the cut edge for folding.[36]

---

[35] Irene Brückle and Jana Dambrogio, "Paper Splitting: History and Modern Technology," *Journal of the American Institute for Conservation* 39, no. 3 (2000): 295–325.

[36] William Berwick's correspondence with I. Minis Hays provides many examples of his relentless search for the perfect tracing cloth: thin, translucent, flexible, and plain white rather than blue white. Various firms stopped manufacturing it, and he was forced to look for other sources—a conundrum that is familiar to today's conservators as well.

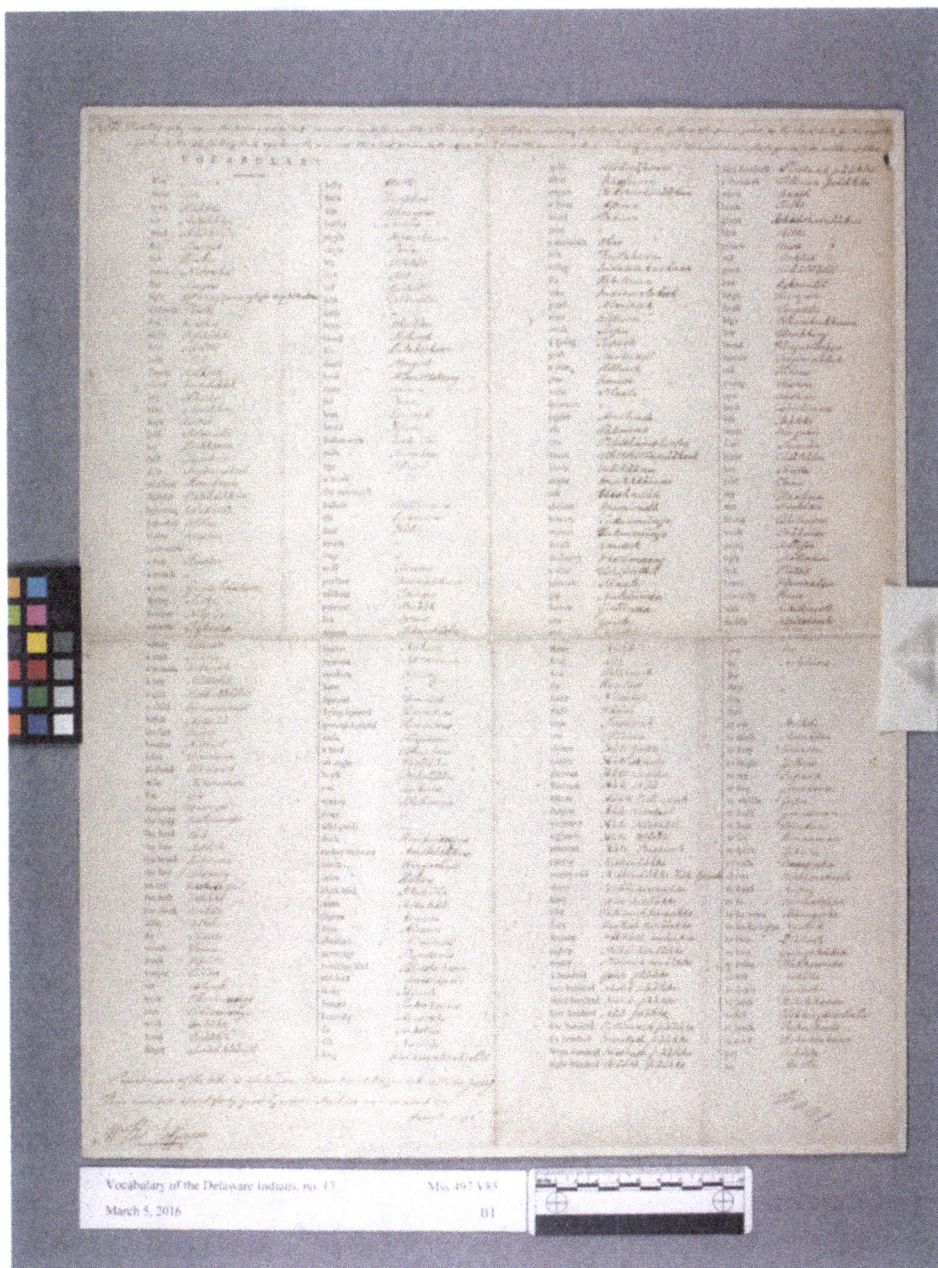

Figure 18a. Vocabulary of the Delaware Indians (fig. 18a) and Vocabulary of the Nanticoke Indians (fig. 18b, overleaf) before re-treatment in 2015–2016. William Berwick split, mounted, and silked the top and bottom halves of these vocabulary forms. The two halves were then hinged together with linen tape or tracing cloth for sewing. Mss.497.V85, American Philosophical Society Historical and Literary Committee, American Indian Vocabulary Collection. Courtesy of Anne Downey.

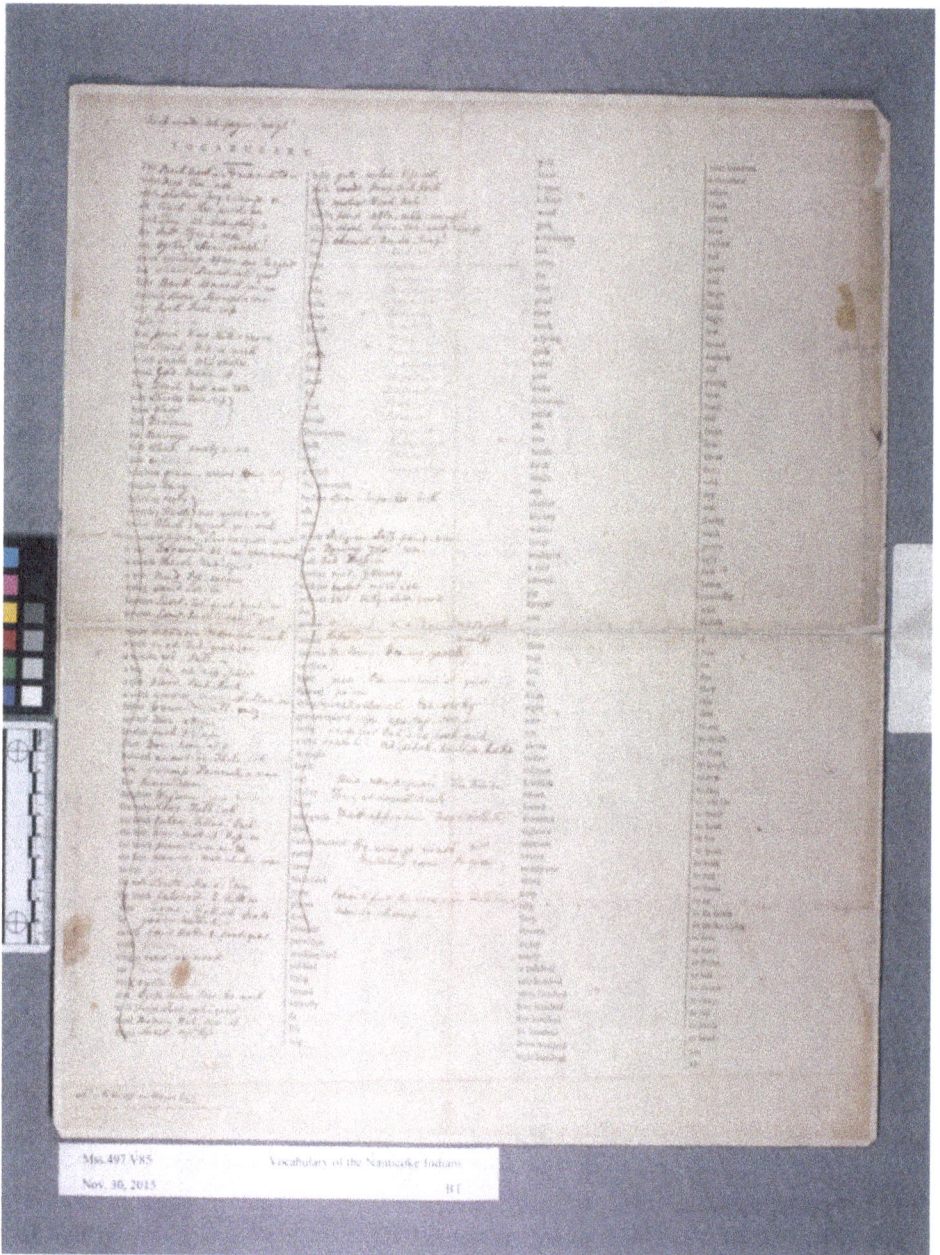

Figure 18b.   Vocabulary of the Nanticoke Indians as treated by William Berwick (see caption on overleaf).

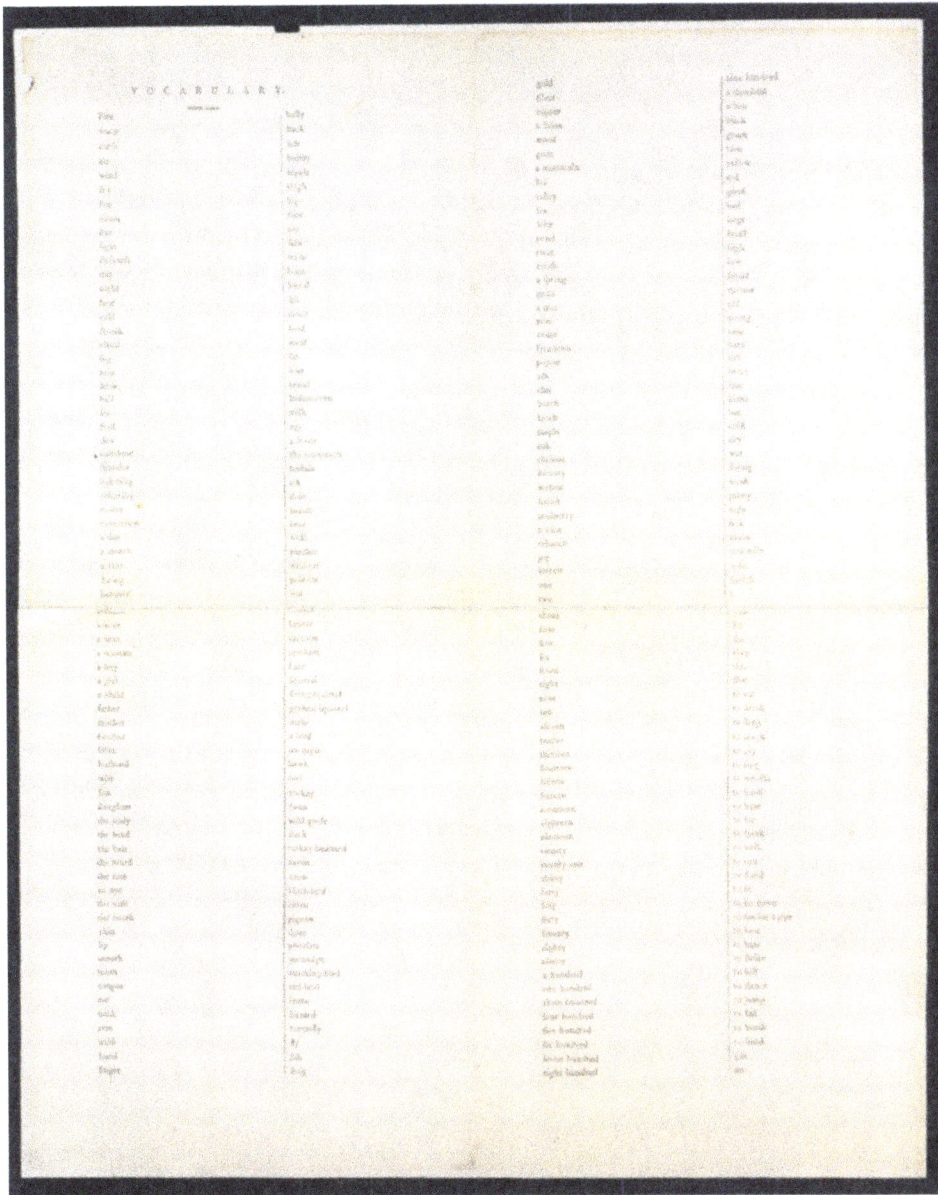

Figure 19. William Berwick split this blank vocabulary form from the filled-in vocabulary for the Delaware Indians, as revealed by the corroded inkblot common to both (see fig. 18a). Mss.497.V85, American Philosophical Society Historical and Literary Committee, American Indian Vocabulary Collection. Courtesy of the American Philosophical Society.

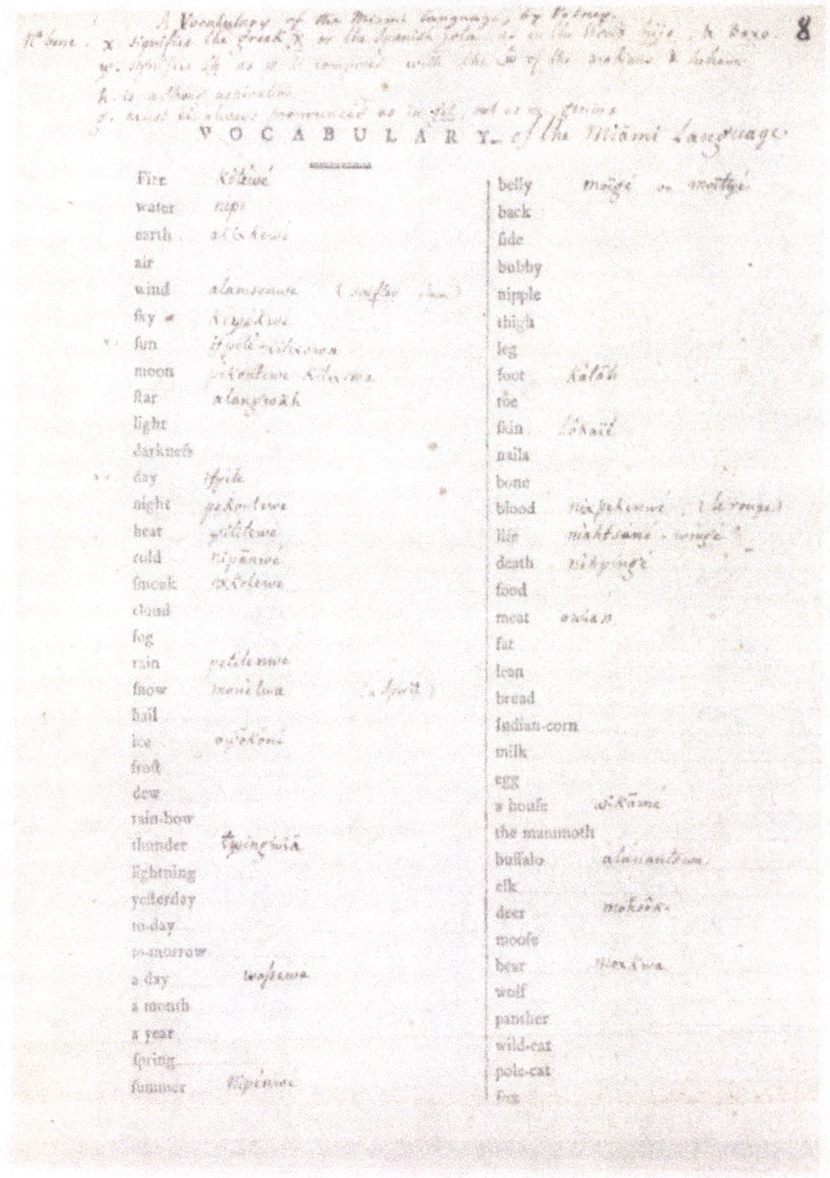
VOCABULARY

Fire	belly
water	back
earth	fide
air	bubby
wind	nipple
fky	thigh
fun	leg
moon	foot
ftar	toe
light	fkin
darknefs	nails
day	bone
night	blood
heat	life
cold	death
fmoak	food
cloud	meat
fog	fat
rain	lean
fnow	bread
hail	Indian-corn
ice	milk
froft	egg
dew	a houfe
rain-bow	the mammoth
thunder	buffalo
lightning	elk
yefterday	deer
to-day	moofe
to-morrow	bear
a day	wolf
a month	panther
a year	wild-cat
fpring	pole-cat
fummer	fox

Figure 20. Top left quarter of the vocabulary form for the Miami Indians. Whereas William Berwick cut the other vocabulary forms in half after mounting, the Miami form was mounted in quarters, perhaps because it had already split along previous folds. The cut horizontal edge of each of the four quarters was provided with a false margin of antique paper to approximate the leaf size of the bound volume for which they were destined. Mss.497.V85, American Philosophical Society Historical and Literary Committee, American Indian Vocabulary Collection. Courtesy of the American Philosophical Society.

Downey continued, "The object was also trimmed along the edges: the bottom of the Jefferson signature has been trimmed away." Given Berwick's frequent insistence that "not a particle of the writing has been injured or lost" (this particular example comes from his letter to I. Minis Hays on November 16, 1903), it seems likely that this trimming was carried out by an earlier binder of the vocabulary lists. Downey observed that the heavy lining paper was "weak and brittle," with dog-eared and torn corners, and that the cloth hinge was also torn. Her 2003 treatment involved reinforcing the hinge and lining paper while leaving the existing restoration intact.

In 2015, both the Delaware and Nanticoke vocabularies were slated for exhibition, this time in the APS Museum's *Gathering Voices: Thomas Jefferson and Native America*. By this time, the lining paper and silk crepeline were markedly weak and brittle, providing inadequate support for the original documents. Downey also tested the iron gall ink on both forms and found that they contained excess iron(II) ions, which can catalyze corrosion of the paper. These findings led Downey to perform a calcium phytate treatment—first proposed by Dutch chemist Han Neevel in 1995—to stabilize the inks. This treatment uses phytic acid, an antioxidant found in certain seeds, to inactivate the oxidative components of iron gall ink. Downey immersed the vocabulary lists in an aqueous calcium phytate bath, during which the silking, lining paper, and residual adhesives were removed. Once the thin handmade paper of the original documents had air-dried, Downey was able to see that both sheets were skinned unevenly across their back surfaces. This, along with the papers' unusual reactions during bathing, led her to conclude that they had been previously faced with "strong gelatin or glue" and split.

Looking through the Berwick-Hays correspondence, which had been uncovered during paper conservator Christine Smith's first research trip to the APS Library around 1998, Downey discovered Berwick's references to splitting the vocabularies. A corroded inkblot common to both sheets allowed her to link the Delaware vocabulary she had just washed with the blank vocabulary form it had been split from (see figs. 18a and 19). With this knowledge in hand, Downey sized the skinned side of the Delaware vocabulary with a dilute gelatin solution to combat its curl from the residual facing adhesive. She then mended both documents with thin, strong, translucent Asian paper, bridging Berwick's cuts along the horizontal folds and returning the forms to single sheets (figs. 21a and 21b). Downey also

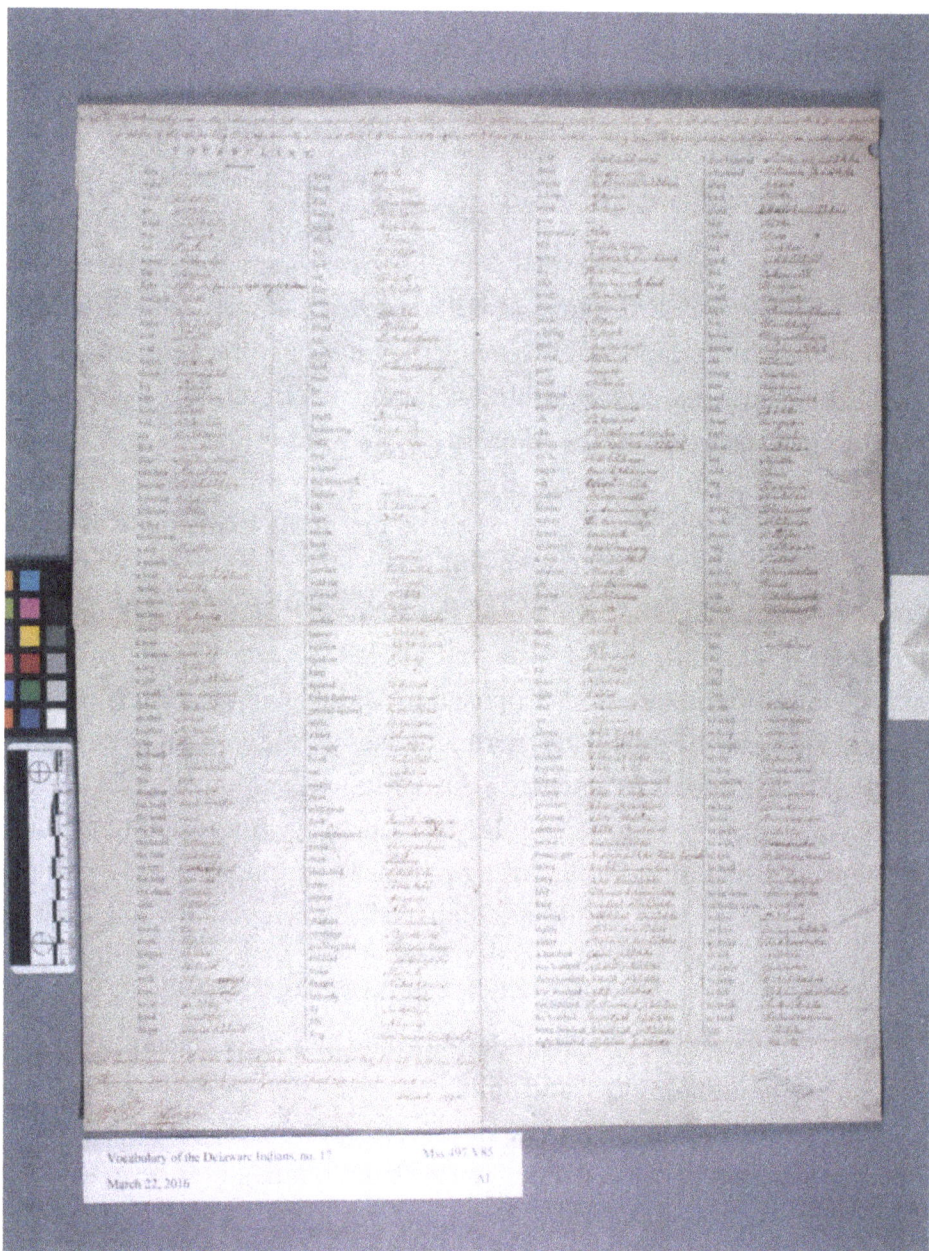

Figure 21a. Vocabulary of the Delaware Indians (fig. 21a) and Vocabulary of the Nanticoke Indians (fig. 21b, facing page) after treatment in 2016. Anne Downey performed calcium phytate treatment on these vocabulary forms in 2015 and 2016, removing William Berwick's brittle mounting systems at the same time. The sheets were mended to form single sheets once more, although they remain half their original thickness. Mss.497.V85, American Philosophical Society Historical and Literary Committee, American Indian Vocabulary Collection. Courtesy of Anne Downey.

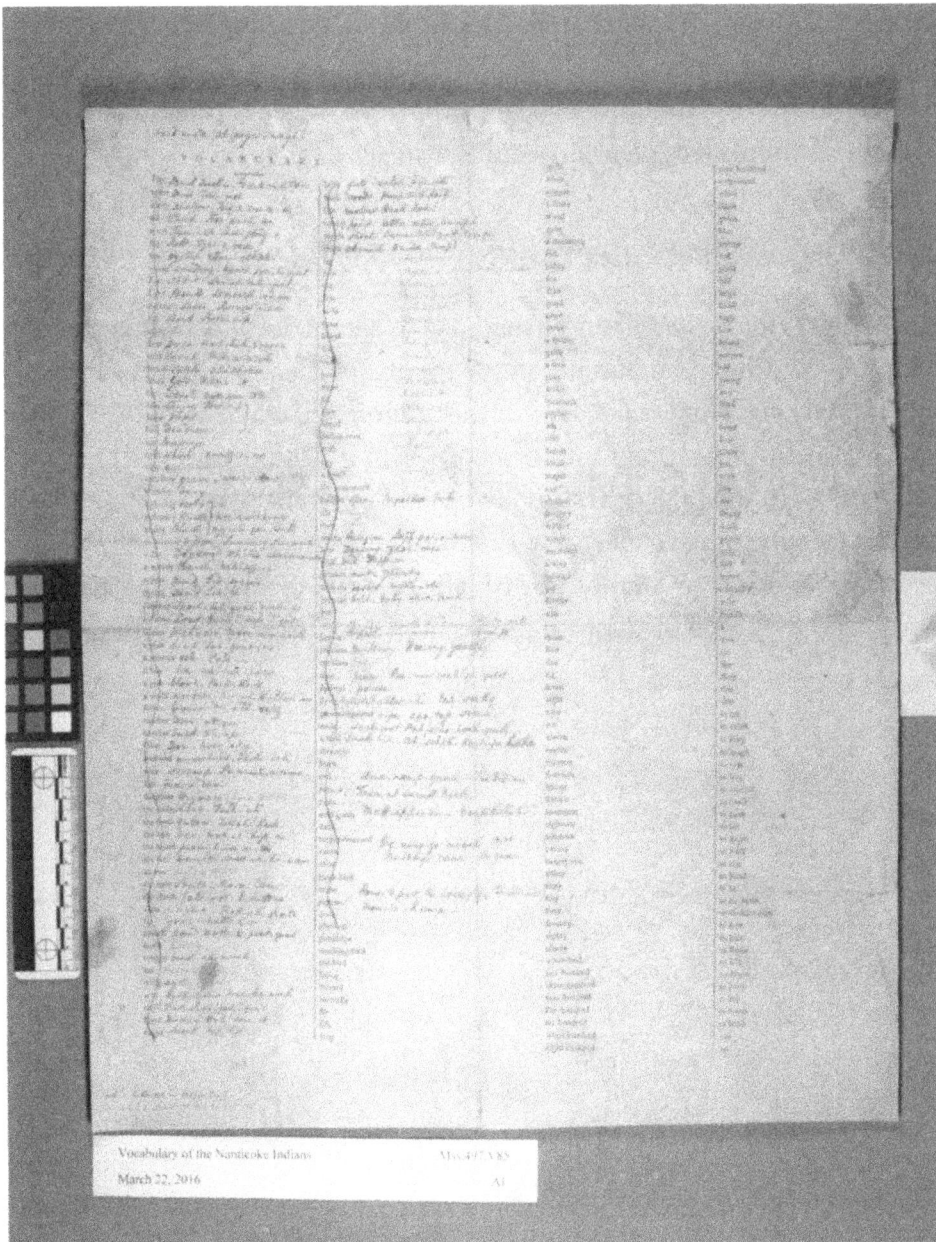

Figure 21b. Vocabulary of the Nanticoke Indians after re-treatment in 2016 (see caption on facing page).

recorded information about Berwick's previous paper-splitting campaign in her treatment reports. Copies of the pertinent letter to Hays now reside with Downey's treatment reports in the objects' folders, providing context for both her treatment decisions and Berwick's.

Charles Willson Peale, Diary Vol. 1, 1765–1767, Mss.B.P31

The earliest Charles Willson Peale diary in the APS collection is a small volume bound in green parchment, 6 × 4 inches, designed to fit comfortably in a pocket. The back cover of the volume once had a fold-over flap whose metal pin snapped into a metal clasp on the front cover to hold the book shut. Peale appears to have used the blank volume not only as a diary (the first leaves describe a 1765 trip to Boston on which he suffered from toothache) but for to-do lists and daily recordkeeping. Several leaves in the middle of the volume recount expenses for food, pigments,

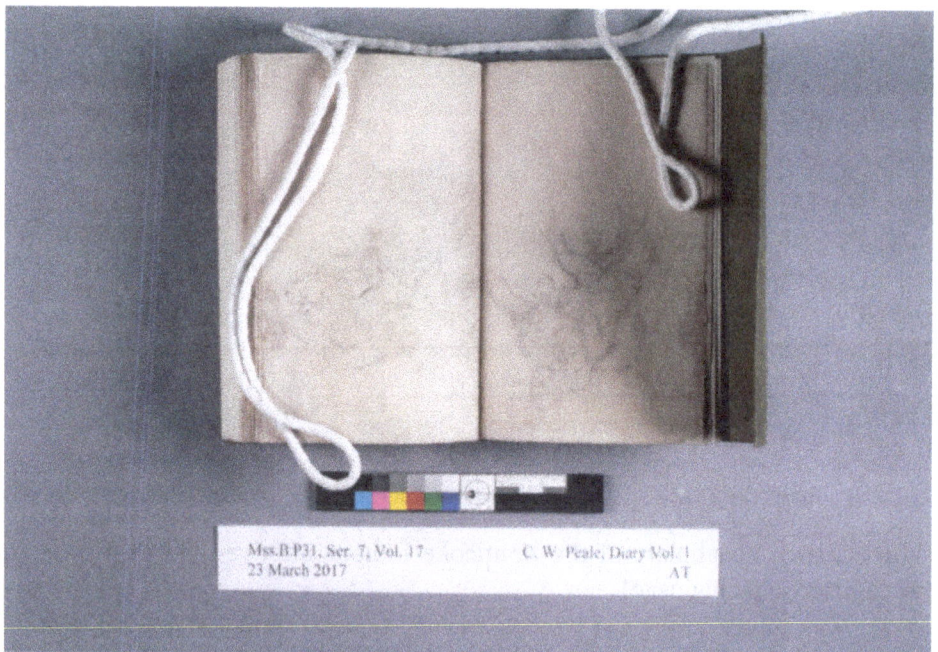

Figure 22. In 1767, Charles Willson Peale hid outside the London room where Benjamin Franklin was fondling a young woman and sketched their activities in his pocket diary. After conservation treatment, these pages were on display in *Curious Revolutionaries*. Mss.B.P31, Peale-Sellers Family Collection, 1686–1963, American Philosophical Society. Courtesy of the author.

and canvas. Other leaves contain technical drawings or sketches of people in ink or graphite.

Two of these pencil sketches date to Peale's 1767 stay in London, where he studied under American expatriate portraitist Benjamin West (1738–1820). During his studies, Peale found his way to Benjamin Franklin's residence and was allowed to enter the house despite his lack of an invitation. From the stairs, Peale spied Franklin in an inner room, busily engaged with a previous visitor. Rather than retreating, he pulled out his pocketbook and documented the scene. The two sketches, made on facing pages of Peale's diary, reveal an aging Franklin holding a young woman on his lap, caressing her hand and kissing her (see fig. 22).

For the APS Museum's 2017 exhibition, *Curious Revolutionaries: The Peales of Philadelphia*, curators wanted to display the diary open to the scandalous sketches, but the volume was initially in no shape to be exhibited. The binding was detached and only the front cover and the torn, crumpled spine remained (see fig. 23). Whereas the spine of the

Figure 23. When Charles Willson Peale's diary arrived in the APS Conservation Department, all that was left of its original parchment binding was this detached front cover with the tattered spine attached. Mss.B.P31, Peale-Sellers Family Collection, 1686–1963, American Philosophical Society. Courtesy of the author.

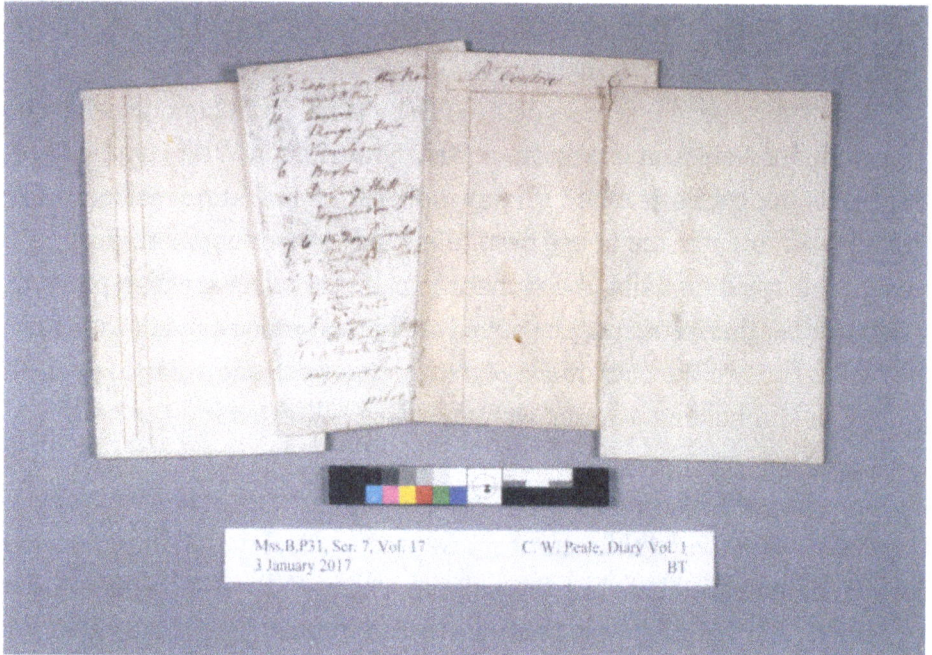

Figure 24. Sometime between 1948 and 2015, the surviving leaves of Charles Willson Peale's diary were guarded and sewn into four thin pamphlets with hard modern sewing thread. The pamphlets on the right exhibit moderate discoloration and staining from moisture and mold. Mss.B.P31, Peale-Sellers Family Collection, 1686–1963, American Philosophical Society. Courtesy of the author.

binding was half an inch thick, the surviving leaves made a pile less than a quarter-inch high, suggesting that much of the original book was missing. Furthermore, the leaves had been reassembled into a set of four small pamphlets during a previous restoration campaign, likely under the direction of Hedi Kyle or Denise Carbone, given the hard, round modern sewing thread that was commonly used at the APS during their tenures (fig. 24). The pages had never been numbered, making the order of the pamphlets—and of the leaves within them—unclear. In one place, Peale had clearly turned his diary sideways to write a poem across two facing pages, but when the leaves were resewn into pamphlets, the two halves of the poem were separated by an unrelated folio of paper (see figs. 25a and 25b). In 2017, the goals of conservation treatment were to determine the original order of the leaves and to rebind them in their original cover, adding new material as necessary to make the book strong and functional.

Several physical and textual clues assisted me in approximating the original order of the diary. Many of the leaves had suffered extensive water

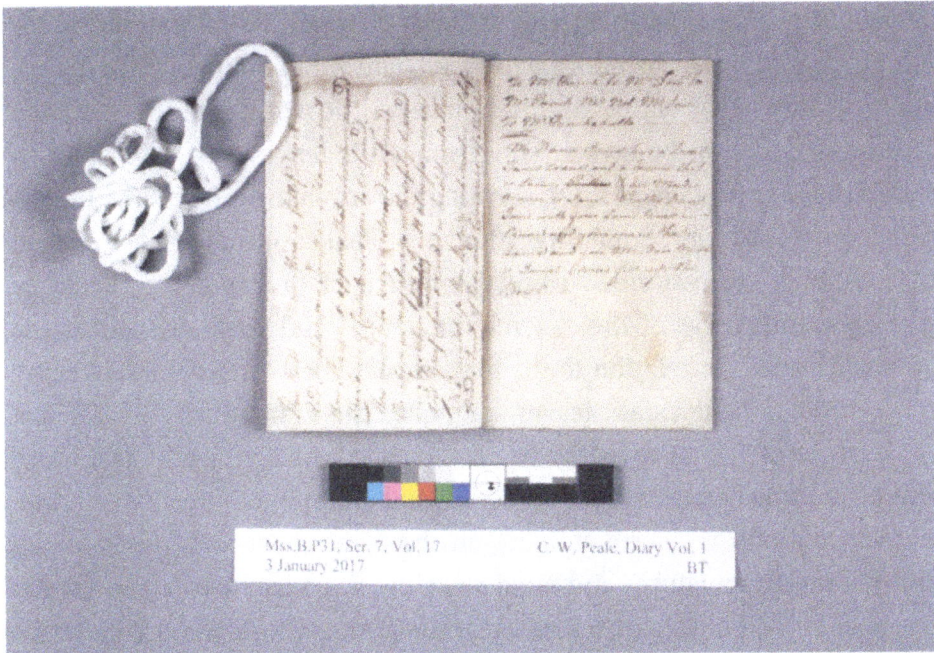

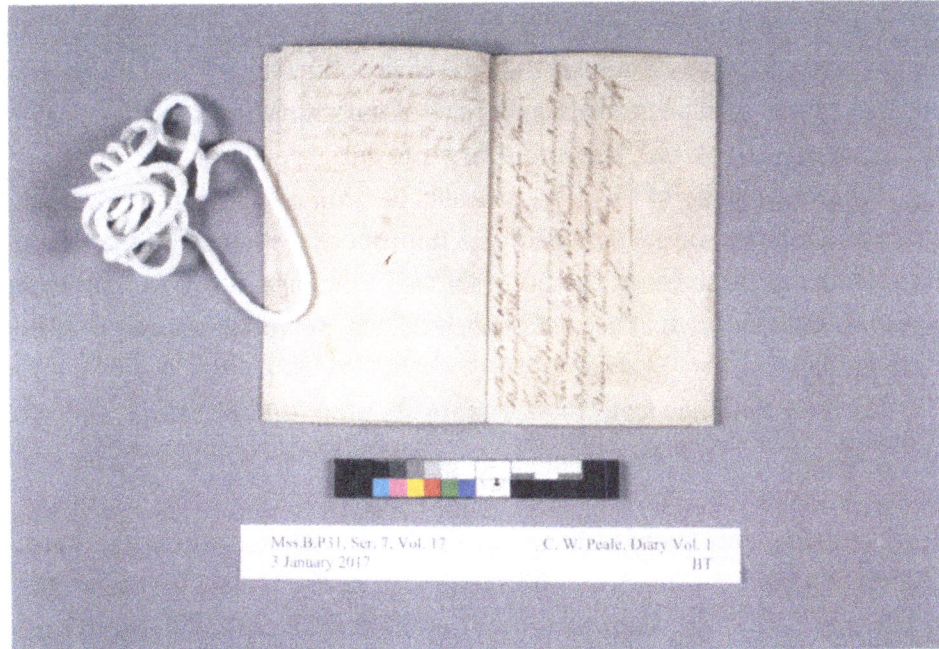

Figures 25a and 25b.   Charles Willson Peale turned his diary sideways to copy Samuel Wesley's popular song lyrics, "The world, my dear Mira, is full of deceit," written in 1784 for the Duchess of Norfolk. The twentieth-century restorer who sewed the diary into pamphlets also misordered its leaves, breaking the song in the middle and preventing it from being read. Mss.B.P31, Peale-Sellers Family Collection, 1686–1963, American Philosophical Society. Courtesy of the author.

damage in the past, with varying degrees of brown discoloration, bleeding ink, marks from rusted straight pins, and mold stains. Other leaves, and the extant cover of the volume, had very little water staining, confined to the very edges of the leaves. The clean, white leaves were also dated to Peale's diary entries from 1765, allowing the surviving cover to be identified as the front cover. Sometime after 1765, Peale appears to have flipped the book over and resumed writing from the back (a common practice for his time), and many of the severely moisture- and mold-stained leaves are upside-down in relation to the first leaves. These observations led me to conclude that the extant leaves composed the first section and the last two sections of the diary, which are dated to 1767. There were most likely several sections between them in the original diary; these are now missing.

The minimal moisture staining on the front cover and leaves, along with the severe moisture- and mold-staining of the last leaves, provided a rationale for the missing back cover of the diary, whose parchment binding would have been extremely susceptible to water damage. The mold and moisture stains also proved to be extremely helpful in reordering the water-damaged leaves. Stains at the fore-edge of the diary could be aligned, and the leaves could be ordered so the size of the stains progressed logically as the pages were turned, becoming larger toward the back cover.

A 1948 microfilm of the diary was also helpful, revealing that the book had already been water damaged and improperly rebound by that date. Mold stains in the back of the book showed that certain leaves had been bound in upside down. The undamaged leaves, however, appeared to be logically ordered.

Based on evidence from the moisture staining, the microfilm, and the text of the surviving diary pages, I numbered the leaves with a soft graphite pencil to correspond to their most likely original order. I then disbound the pamphlets and mended the spine folds of the folios where the hard, thin thread from the previous treatment had cut the paper. I replaced the missing portion of the diary with sections of blank alkaline paper to return the book to its original dimensions (see fig. 26). I then re-sewed the reordered book block with two plies of soft linen thread, which was commonly used in the hand-binding period both to prevent damage to the spine folds of the paper and to avoid adding unnecessary thickness at the spine of the book. I rebound the pocketbook using the original front cover and spine,

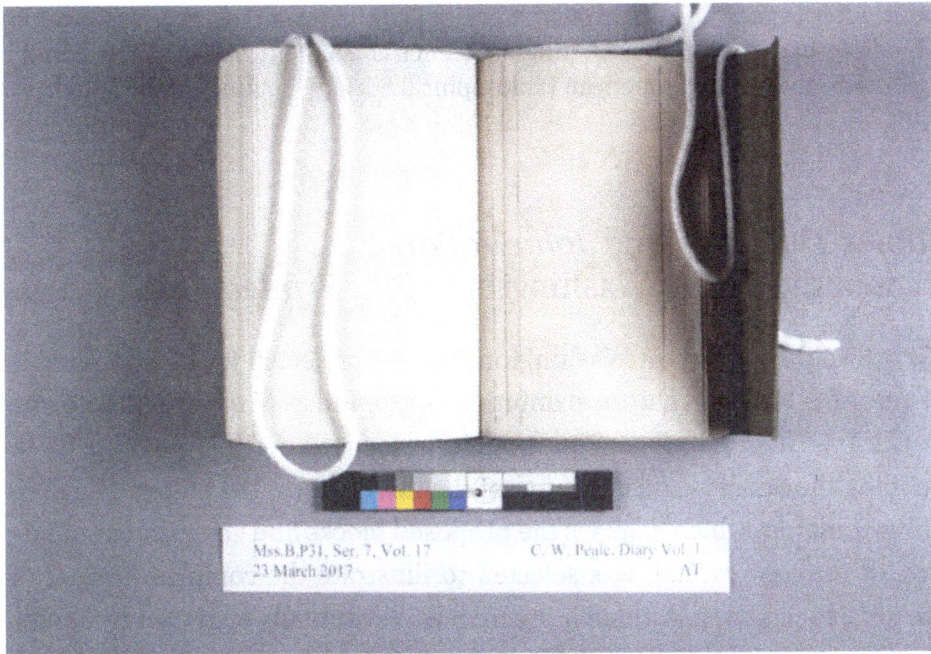

Figure 26. Conservation treatment for Charles Willson Peale's diary included inserting new leaves of modern paper at the middle of the book to replace the leaves that have been lost. Here, the new leaves appear on the left, while the surviving mold-stained leaves from the back of the book are visible on the right. Mss.B.P31, Peale-Sellers Family Collection, 1686–1963, American Philosophical Society. Courtesy of the author.

which I stabilized with acrylic-toned Asian paper reinforcements. I also created a new back cover with a fore-edge flap from alkaline cardstock covered with acrylic-toned handmade Western paper (see fig. 27). These repair materials have been tested for their chemical and physical stability, and they restore the binding to wholeness while being easily differentiated from the original parchment.

My photographic and written documentation for the project provides evidence of the book's previous binding campaigns and of my rationale for redoing the work. In this case, both the erroneous page order and the damaging sewing thread provided compelling reasons for re-treatment. Repairing and reusing the book's original binding also restored some of its historical context, giving researchers and museum viewers a better understanding of how Peale would have used the volume.

Figure 27. A new back cover and fore-edge envelope flap for the diary were created using alkaline cardstock and handmade Western paper toned with acrylic paint. After conservation treatment, Charles Willson Peale's diary can be read in a binding that approximates its original format. Mss.B.P31, Peale-Sellers Family Collection, 1686–1963, American Philosophical Society. Courtesy of the author.

James Thackara and John Vallance, Plan of the City of Washington, 1792, *Printed.Maps*

A 1792 engraved map of Washington, DC, was selected for display as part of the APS Museum's 2019 exhibition, *Mapping a Nation: Shaping the Early American Republic*. This exhibition focused on the role of maps in defining the borders and character of the fledgling United States. The map of Washington, which displays the proposed blocks and government buildings of the new capital, was selected to illustrate the complex process of creating such a map. Although the map was eventually engraved by James Thackara and John Vallance of Philadelphia, Andrew Ellicott (1754–1820) led the surveying team that compiled the information leading to the map. In 1784, Ellicott had assisted David Rittenhouse in extending the survey of the Mason-Dixon line. From 1791 to 1792, he surveyed the proposed District of

Columbia and Federal City for Secretary of State Thomas Jefferson, aided by free Black astronomer and surveyor Benjamin Banneker (1731–1806). The exhibition noted that Banneker was paid less than other team members and had to eat separately, illustrating some of the ways in which people of color were marginalized during nation-building. The final map incorporates the work of all these men, as well as the earlier work of city planner Pierre Charles L'Enfant (1754–1825).

The Society's copy of the map was presented by David Stewart Erskine (1742–1829), 11th Earl of Buchan, a Scottish antiquarian and supporter of the American Revolution who had received the map from George Washington. His holograph iron gall ink inscription along the right edge of the map reinforces the white, male, Eurocentric power structure of the emerging nation:

> This Plan which was sent to me by the illustrious Washington April 22 1793, I dedicate to the memory of C. Columbus, B. de las Casas, Sir W. Raleigh, W. Penn, John Locke, Benjamin Franklin, Samuel Adams, John Hancock, Generals Warren and Montgomery, and to that of all the good and brave men who contributed to the establishment of American Happiness and I bequeath this plan to the Phil. Society of America instituted Jan: 2d. 1769.

Above Buchan's dedication is a slip of bluish paper bearing the inscription "G Washington to the Earl of Buchan." Buchan apparently cut the autograph from the letter originally accompanying the map, as it is densely written on the opposite side, and secured it to the map with a dot of adhesive. When the front of the map was silked overall sometime after its arrival at the APS in 1802, possibly by Carol Rugh or Willman Spawn, the slip was removed from the map (creating a hole in the inscription), silked separately, and re-adhered on top of the silk-laminated map.

By the time the map was selected for exhibition, it displayed multiple long cracks (perhaps the original reason for silking), losses filled with white and brown papers, and several edge tears. It was also markedly discolored, particularly at the top left edge, which was stained brown (see fig. 28). The Library's iron gall ink inscription marking the 1802 receipt of the map was also haloed, indicating an early stage of ink corrosion. These condition issues were judged severe enough to warrant calcium phytate treatment to stabilize the inks and bathing to reduce the staining and discoloration. To prevent further damage to Washington's signature, the attached slip was detached from the map prior to bathing,

Figure 28.   James Thackara and John Vallance, *Plan of the City of Washington, 1792,* Printed Maps Collection, American Philosophical Society. Before treatment, the map was discolored overall, with significant staining at the top left corner. The 1802 iron gall ink inscription was also haloed. The map was likely silked by Carol Rugh or Willman Spawn in the twentieth century. Courtesy of Anisha Gupta.

using a scalpel to break the weak adhesive join. The remainder of the silk was readily removed during bathing (see fig. 29). In this case, even though removal of the silk lamination was not one of the goals of treatment, the previous conservation effort was reversed in hopes of improving the map's legibility.

After bathing, the map was mended again with Japanese paper and toned cast paper pulp. Washington's untreated signature was hinged to the map in its former location with Asian paper and wheat starch paste—a reversible and chemically stable adhesive—with its silk lamination still in place (see fig. 30). The silk from the remainder of the map was labeled with graphite and retained in the conservation lab as a piece of historical evidence. Even though no earlier conservation records exist for this map, its previous lamination and mends are noted in the treatment report that now accompanies the object.

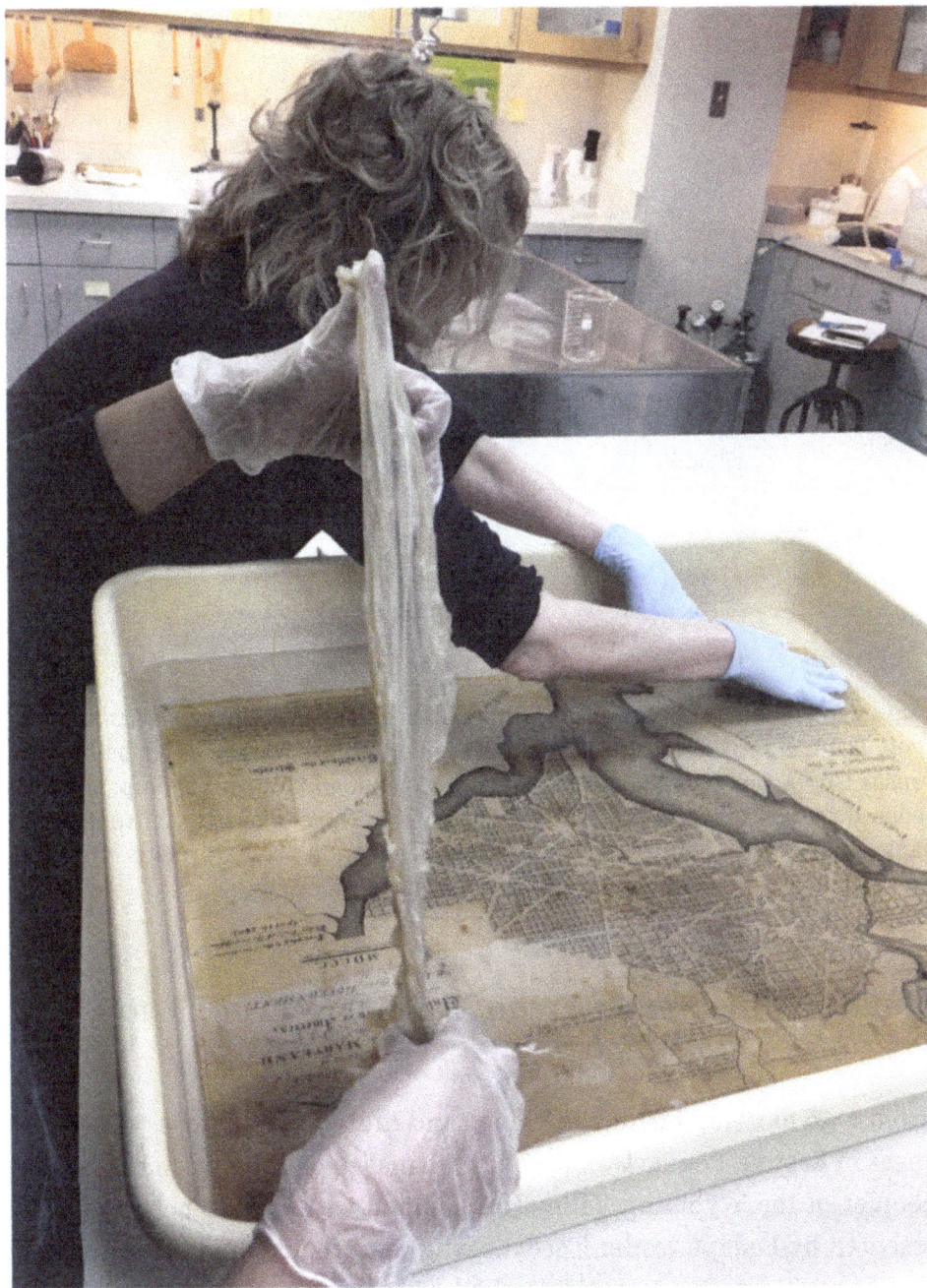

Figure 29. James Thackara and John Vallance, *Plan of the City of Washington, 1792*, Printed Maps Collection, American Philosophical Society. Anisha Gupta and Anne Downey performed calcium phytate treatment on the map to stabilize the iron gall ink and reduce staining. Even though removing its silk lamination was not one of the goals of treatment, the silk released readily in the bath, and its removal improves the legibility of the treated map. Courtesy of the author.

Figure 30. James Thackara and John Vallance, *Plan of the City of Washington, 1792*, Printed Maps Collection, American Philosophical Society. After bathing it, Anisha Gupta mended the map with Japanese paper and toned cast pulp. She also reduced the worst of the residual staining with a cosmetic overlay of translucent Japanese paper. The untreated slip bearing Washington's signature was hinged to the map in its former location. Courtesy of Anne Downey.

Minutes of the Indian Treaty Council Held at Easton, 1757, Mss.970.5.M659.1

From 1756 to 1758, during the French and Indian War, a series of conferences in Easton, Pennsylvania, sought to make peace between the Native peoples of the Wyoming Valley (often allied with the French, and represented by Lenape leader Teedyuscung) and the colonial government. The Lenape people in particular had been at war with Pennsylvanian colonizers since the fraudulent 1737 Walking Purchase forced them from their homeland in the Lehigh Valley to the Wyoming Valley, traditionally controlled by the Iroquois. The Iroquois, who were allied with the British, subsequently sold the land upon which the Lenape had settled to Pennsylvania and Connecticut, sparking violent hostilities between the Lenape and Pennsylvanian settlers.

Teedyuscung aired Lenape grievances at the first treaty councils in 1756, and he elaborated upon them in 1757, asking for a colonial secretary to take down his words. Charles Thomson, who later became clerk of the Continental Congress, was appointed to serve in that role. The council meetings held between July 21 and August 7, 1757, concluded in a peace treaty between the Pennsylvania government and the Lenape, but the treaty did not return Lenape land or end the colony's conflict with other Native groups. A more widespread peace was struck during the final Treaty of Easton in 1758, which returned some of the land taken from the Iroquois and pledged that British settlers would not trespass on Native lands in the Ohio region west of the Allegheny Mountains. These treaties created a tenuous alliance between the British colonial government and local tribes that had previously supported the French.

The APS now holds later copies of the minutes from the 1756 Easton treaties, believed to be produced between 1780 and 1820, and these were treated by Carol Rugh in 1935. Far more importantly, the Society also preserves Charles Thomson's original manuscript minutes from 1757, representing Lenape land claims with maps based on Teedyuscung's own sketch of the debated territories and a contemporary British map of Pennsylvania drawn by Lewis Evans. These minutes—apparently a first draft based on Thomson's rough notes—were subsequently bound in multiple oversewing campaigns. The minutes' original binding may not survive; the undated finding aid for the collection describes a "half morocco [binding], covers detached, and a few leaves loose." This description may refer to a nineteenth-century half binding of purple embossed sheepskin with marbled paper sides, whose boards were stored with the volume throughout its complicated treatment history.

According to Denise Carbone's later treatment notes, Willman Spawn mended and guarded the minutes during his career, sometime after 1950, and rebound them in a three-piece case binding covered with green paper. This binding remained on the book until 2004, when the volume was disbound and partially treated in preparation for the Society's 2005 *Treasures Revealed* exhibition. Carbone's notes from disbinding, which remained with the book until treatment was completed in 2019, mentioned the book's single-folio endleaves of stiff paper and extraordinarily wide guards, or strips of repair paper joining the leaves together in the gutter. These guards were apparently designed to allow the book to be oversewn without damage to the original manuscript. Treatment photographs found on the APS servers show that the guards (apparently of a soft bond paper) were lined with silk that extended onto the manuscript leaves for about an inch on each side. In the years after Spawn conserved the book, the silk lamination became stiff and brittle, and the treaty minutes cracked throughout the book block adjacent to the silk (see fig. 31). Carbone also

Figure 31. Minutes of the Indian Treaty Council Held at Easton, 1757, Mss.970.5.M659.1, American Philosophical Society. By 2004, Willman Spawn's silk-laminated guards had stiffened, causing the leaves of the minutes to crack along the edge of the silk. Courtesy of Denise Carbone.

noted extensive tide lines or moisture stains on the manuscript leaves, generally along the gutter edges, probably resulting from the earlier silking
treatment (see fig. 32). Carbone disbound the manuscript leaves, which
also displayed extensive iron gall ink corrosion, with cracking and dropout
(see fig. 33), and turned them over to Anne Downey for paper treatment.

Figure 32. Minutes of the Indian Treaty Council Held at Easton, 1757,
Mss.970.5.M659.1, American Philosophical Society. In this 2004 treatment photograph, a severe tide line can be seen extending from Willman Spawn's guard
and silk lamination, suggesting that his rice starch paste allowed components of
the iron gall ink to move laterally within the paper. Such tide lines were common
throughout the book block prior to washing. Courtesy of Denise Carbone.

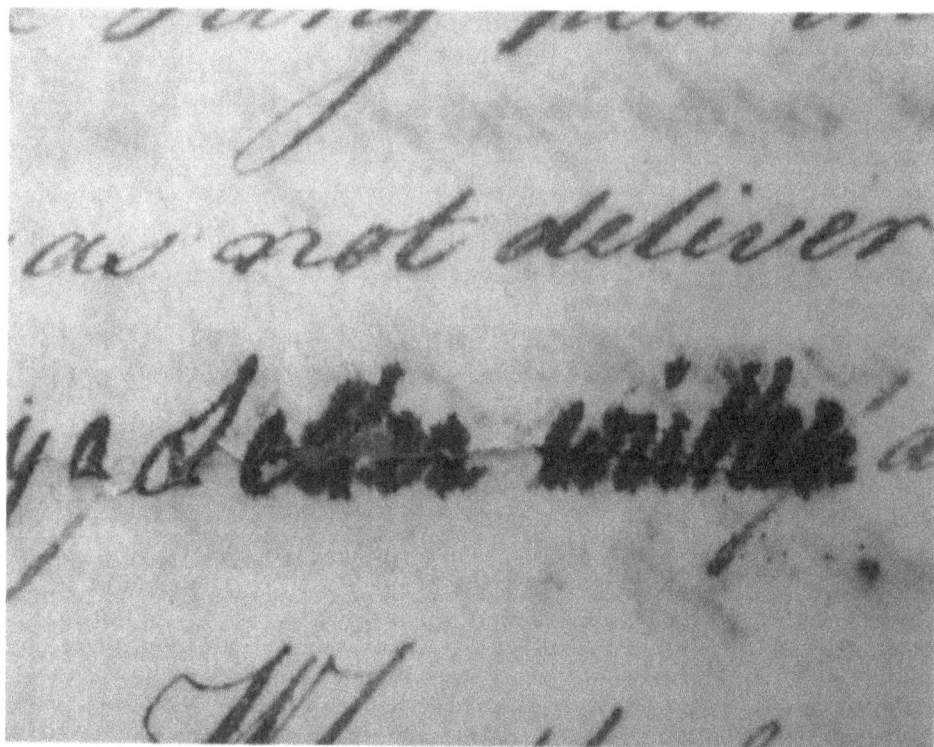

Figure 33. Minutes of the Indian Treaty Council Held at Easton, 1757, Mss.970.5.M659.1, American Philosophical Society. The minutes displayed severe iron gall ink corrosion prior to bathing in 2014, with cracking and dropout where the ink was heavily applied. Courtesy of Denise Carbone.

To address the leaves' discoloration, brittleness, and staining, Downey bathed them in ethanol- and pH-adjusted water, alkalized them to slow acidic deterioration, and sized them with dilute methyl cellulose—a reversible and chemically stable adhesive—to strengthen them. She removed the silk and existing paper mends in the bath. She then mended the leaves with acrylic-toned Asian paper and wheat starch paste. Although calcium phytate treatment might have been appropriate for the manuscript, the Society was not yet using that technique in 2004. (The Library of Congress began testing calcium phytate treatment in 2002; the APS has been using Downey's protocols for the treatment since 2007.) In 2019, when the manuscript's iron gall inks were tested with dampened bathophenanthroline test strips—which Han Neevel developed to indicate the presence of oxidative iron components in ink—the strips remained white or turned a barely perceptible pink. These results suggest that most of the excess iron(II) ions

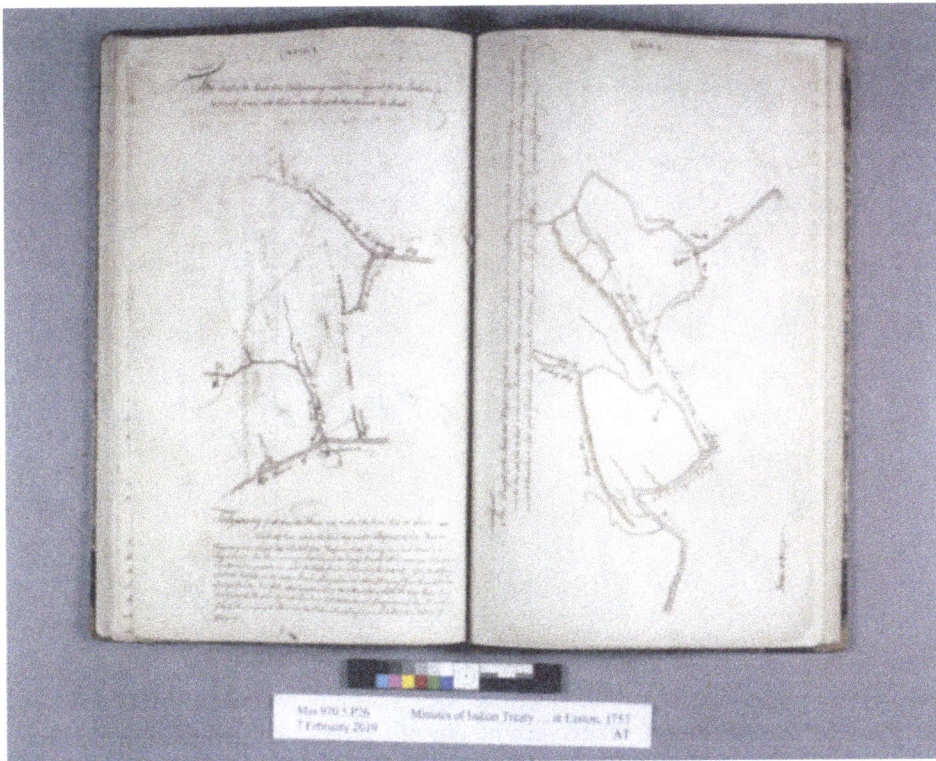

Figure 34. Minutes of the Indian Treaty Council Held at Easton, 1757, Mss.970.5.M659.1, American Philosophical Society. Maps on facing pages of the minutes—featuring Native and colonial depictions of the traditional Lenape lands—were displayed in 2019's *Mapping a Nation*, for which the book was returned to a bound format. Courtesy of the author.

contributing to strikethrough and cracking of the ink were washed away during bathing. Bathing also served to reduce the extensive tide lines and staining throughout the book.

Two leaves from the minutes were displayed separately during the 2005 exhibition, and the book was not returned to a bound format until 2019, when it was again slated for display in *Mapping a Nation*. The curators requested that the book be shown intact because the maps for exhibition appeared on facing pages (fig. 34). In order to preserve the manuscript's original format to the extent possible, I examined the leaves' watermarks to determine how they had originally been gathered, or divided into separate sections of nested, folded sheets. Handmade paper often has two marks on each sheet, created by different wire embellishments attached to each half of the screen-like mold used to create the paper. Both the main watermark

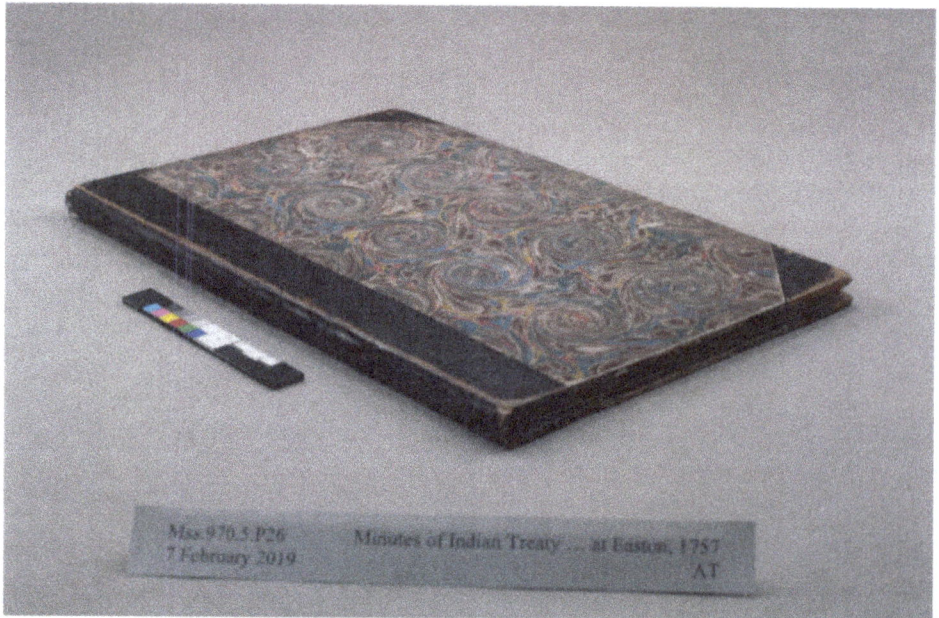

Figure 35. Minutes of the Indian Treaty Council Held at Easton, 1757, Mss.970.5.M659.1, American Philosophical Society. The minutes were rebound in the earliest binding surviving to them, with nineteenth-century half-bound boards and a new spine of laminated cotton and paper. Courtesy of the author.

(often pictorial) and the smaller countermark (often a series of initials) are visible in transmitted light as thinner places in the body of the paper. In the case of the minutes from Easton, the orientations of the watermarks and countermarks showed that the leaves had not been stacked and folded into a group of nested folios known as a quire, as was common practice. Instead, the sheets were written and bound as individual folios of paper.

Based on this evidence, I guarded the leaves into their original folios, provided them with new endleaves of handmade paper, and sewed them through the fold over ramie-ribbon supports. After discussion with the curators, I rebound the minutes in the surviving nineteenth-century boards—the earliest extant binding materials remaining to them—with a new spine of toned, laminated Asian paper and airplane cotton (fig. 35). All of the previous treatments were described in the final report, and Willman Spawn's green paper quarter case binding was provided with a four-flap wrapper and stored in the box with the treated book. The recovered paper treatment form was also scanned as a PDF, and with the earlier treatment photos it was added to the digital conservation archive for the minutes.

Benjamin Franklin, Ledger A and B, 1730–1740, Mss.B.F85f6.5

In 1730, when 24-year-old Benjamin Franklin began keeping his financial records in a tall, narrow leather-bound book labeled "Leidger A" and "Leidger B," he had already moved to Philadelphia, created a discussion group of local businessmen known as the Junto (precursor to today's APS), and begun publishing *The Pennsylvania Gazette* newspaper to promote his ideas and observations. In September 1730, he began a common-law marriage with Deborah Read, and their hands are almost the only ones found in the pages of the ledger book, which contains their financial transactions over the following decade. During these years, Franklin brought his young son William into the new household, wrote the charter for the Library Company of Philadelphia, began publishing *Poor Richard's Almanack*, and established the Union Fire Company. He and Deborah also began a family but lost their son to smallpox.

Little of this personal history is directly reflected in the content of the book, which is concerned with the credits and debts of the Franklin household. As was common at a time when books and paper were costly, the couple kept two systems of accounting in the same binding: a daily journal of transactions at the front of the book and a ledger of transactions indexed by client at the back of the book. When the ledger at the back became full, they began using the remaining blank leaves in the middle of the book. The book was not strictly business, however: One of the last leaves shows Franklin's experimentation with different varieties of iron gall ink, providing evidence for his scientific bent (fig. 36).

Ledger A and B is the earliest Franklin account book known to survive and has long been recognized as one of the treasures of the APS manuscript collection. Shortly after joining the Society in 1935, Carol Rugh picked up where William Berwick had left off and treated seven of Franklin's manuscript record books, including Ledger A and B. Her treatment notes for the volume state, "Loose leather cover attached. Boards stiffened where broken down. Extensive repairs to torn pages. 1 double fold covered with chiffon, hinged & replaced in book" (9). The unsigned slip she pasted into the back of the book provides further (albeit minimal) detail: "page repairs; leather cover strengthened and repaired 6/35" (see fig. 37).

Ledger A and B was not treated again until 2019, almost eighty-five years after Rugh's repairs were made. For many years, the volume had been handled

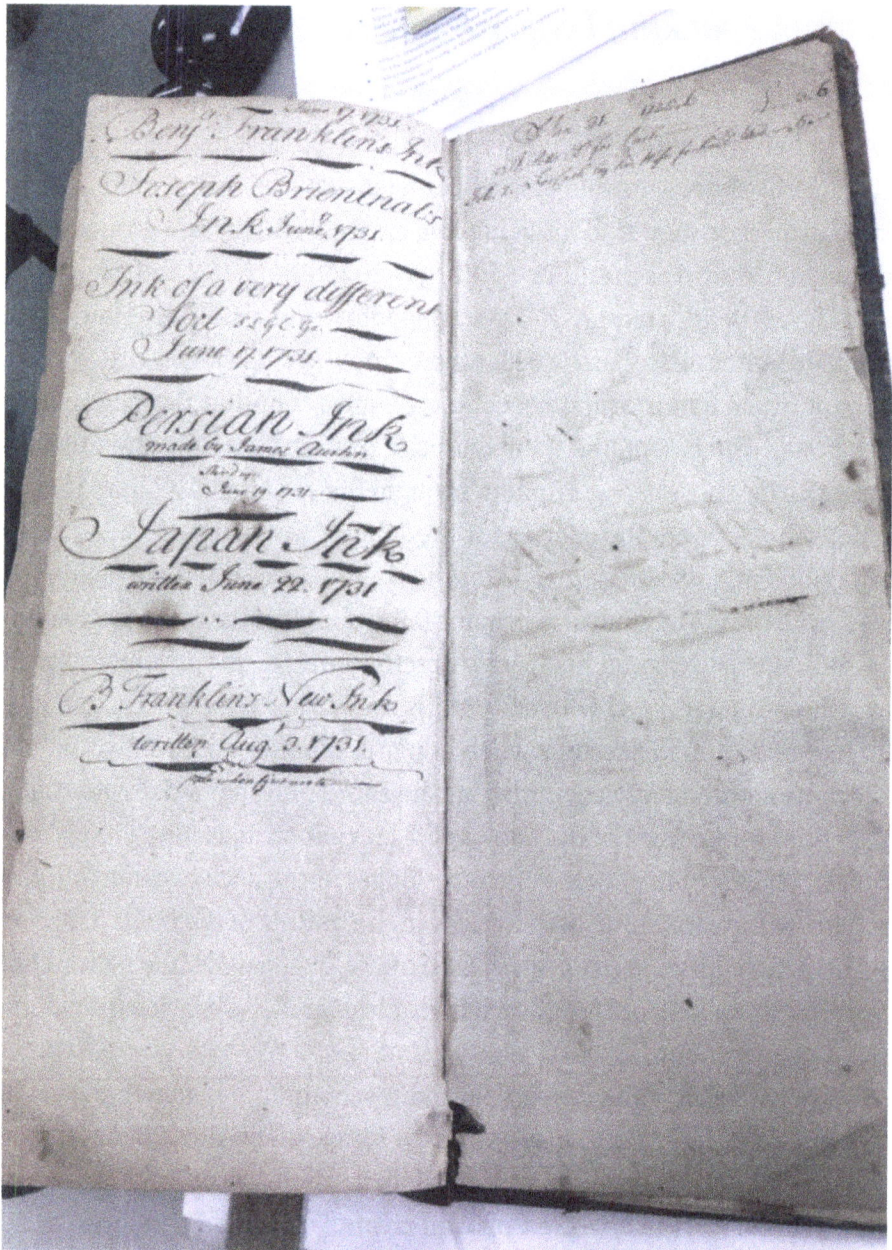

Figure 36. Benjamin Franklin, Ledger A and B, 1730–1740, Mss.B.F85.f6.5, American Philosophical Society. One of the last leaves of the ledger book displays a dated list of different iron gall ink recipes, including Benja. Franklin's Ink, Joseph Brientnal's Ink, Ink of a very different sort, Persian Ink made by James Austin, Japan Ink, and B. Franklin's New Ink, all presumably part of an experiment on Franklin's part. Courtesy of the author.

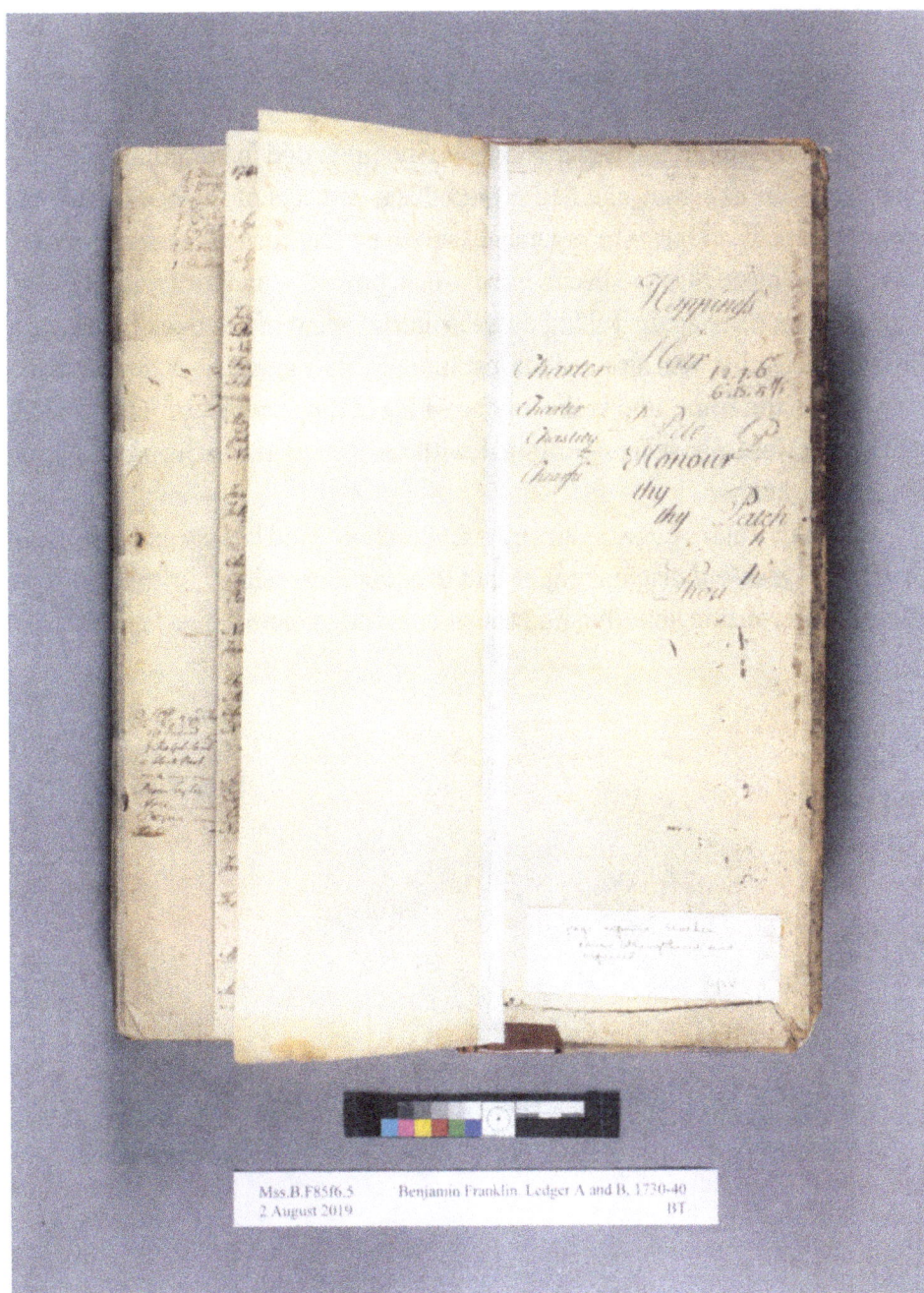

Figure 37. Carol Rugh's 1936 treatment slip for Franklin Ledger A and B, adhered to the back pastedown, states that she made page repairs and strengthened and repaired the leather cover, but it does not specify the materials used. Benjamin Franklin, Ledger A and B, 1730–1740, Mss.B.F85.f6.5, American Philosophical Society. Courtesy of the author.

regularly during tours featuring the Society's most noteworthy collections, and the extensive use had taken its toll. When the book was brought to conservation for treatment, Rugh's identity remained unknown, but examination revealed details about her repairs that were not included in her minimal treatment notes. In this case, she had replaced the endcaps of the book not with chrome-tanned calf but with vegetable-tanned leather turned in over the pastedowns, and by 2019 it had become red, weak, powdery, and torn (fig. 38). The endcaps were once again pulling away from the spine of the book block, and the original leather was also split or lost in many new areas: over the joints, at the center of the spine, and at the top fore-edge of the front board. The corners of the cover were also severely abraded, with associated loss to the pasteboards beneath the leather.

Although Rugh's page repairs remained strong (and largely invisible), the nearly 200-year-old original paper had become increasingly brittle and discolored, and routine handling had caused new edge tears, chips, and creases

Figure 38. By the time Ledger A and B was treated again in 2019, the vegetable-tanned leather Carol Rugh had used to repair its endcaps was weak, red, powdery, and torn. There was also new damage to the leather over the joints and front board. Benjamin Franklin, Ledger A and B, 1730–1740, Mss.B.F85.f6.5, American Philosophical Society. Courtesy of the author.

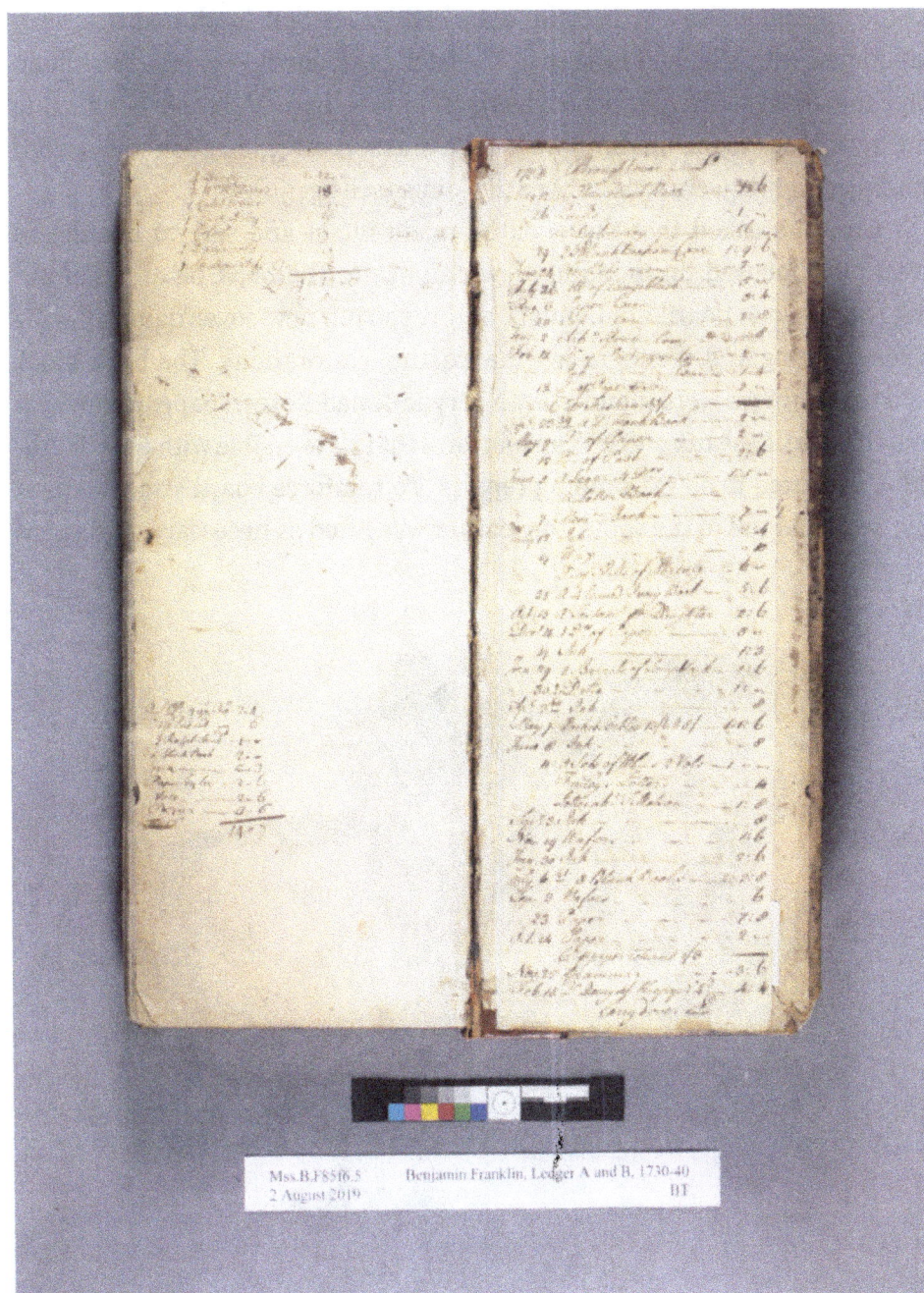

Figure 39.   Before treatment in 2019, the inner hinges of Ledger A and B were split, and several of the sewing supports were broken over the joints, making board attachment tenuous. Here, the split back hinge is shown adjacent to two detached leaves that Carol Rugh trimmed, mended, silked, and hinged to the back pastedown. Benjamin Franklin, Ledger A and B, 1730–1740, Mss.B.F85.f6.5, American Philosophical Society. Courtesy of the author.

in the outermost leaves. The two detached leaves that Rugh had trimmed, laminated with silk, and hinged to the back pastedown with a strip of linen tape remained securely attached, but both inner hinges (the paper connecting the book block to the binding) were split, and several of the book's fiber-cord sewing supports were broken over the joints (see fig. 39).

Curators asked that the book be made intact and safe to handle, so treatment focused on mending new damage to the book block, reinforcing the tenuous board attachment, and repairing new cover damage while strengthening and reintegrating the existing restorations. The book block and inner hinges were mended with acrylic-toned Korean paper and wheat starch paste. Lascaux 498 HV, an adhesive that is reversible with heat or ethanol, was used in all the binding repairs. To reinforce board attachment at the head and tail of the spine, the leather was lifted as necessary, and strips

Figure 40. During treatment in 2019, board attachment was reinforced by adhering strips of ramie ribbon across the spine and over the boards under the leather, separated from the original materials by a reversibility layer of Asian paper and wheat starch paste. Benjamin Franklin, Ledger A and B, 1730–1740, Mss.B.F85.f6.5, American Philosophical Society. Courtesy of the author.

Figure 41.   Carol Rugh's existing leather repairs were not removed in the most recent conservation treatment of Ledger A and B, but they were mended and reinforced, as were new instances of leather damage. The restored book can now be safely handled on tours of the APS treasures. Benjamin Franklin, Ledger A and B, 1730–1740, Mss.B.F85.f6.5, American Philosophical Society. Courtesy of the author.

of ramie ribbon were adhered to the spine and boards over a reversibility layer of Korean *hanji*, or handmade mulberry paper (see fig. 40). The deteriorated endcaps from Rugh's treatment campaign were not removed, but they were reinforced with new, chemically stable components. A loss in the headcap was filled using layers of cotton textile and cotton blotter, and both modern endcaps were faced with acrylic-toned *hanji*. New losses and splits in the boards and original leather were filled and mended with the same materials. After local toning of the leather mends, the binding appears to be intact once more and is safe to handle on tours (see fig. 41). Rugh's repairs remain in place beneath the new materials, as do her exposed turn-ins and her repair slip on the back pastedown. Her role in the conservation history of the book, which was only uncovered during the research for this book, will be added to the existing treatment report.

CHAPTER 4

Considerations for the Re-Treatment of Library Materials

Although the Society's long history of binding, restoration, and conservation may be unique, all libraries contain previously repaired books and documents. Sometimes the earlier binders and restorers are known to the present conservators, and sometimes the repair materials themselves are the only evidence for earlier approaches to collections care. In addition, whereas museums generally rely on program-trained conservators, many libraries have continued to employ binders and book artists trained in artisanal practices, whose knowledge of chemistry, materials science, and conservation ethics sometimes lags behind their peers'. Book owners and donors also frequently take repairs into their own hands, employing everything from pressure-sensitive tape to bathtub bathing. These complex histories of repair should be assessed whenever a previously treated artifact is slated for conservation.

It should be noted that when the preceding treatments were undertaken at the APS, the Society's conservation department had no established protocol for interrogating the significance of prior repairs, documenting them, or retaining historic repair materials. In performing these treatments, the present conservators approached former repairs as they would approach any other aspect of an object's history. They documented the prior treatments in their reports, but some repair materials were kept for future reference, whereas others were stored with the objects or discarded. The general approach to these treatments may be summed up as follows:

- Prior repairs were left intact unless they caused physical or chemical harm, posed a handling risk, or introduced errors that might mislead a user.

- Prior repairs that were visually distracting might be removed or disguised prior to exhibition.
- Prior repairs might also be removed as the side effect of conservation treatment designed to stabilize new chemical or physical damage.
- Where re-treatment was necessary, all prior repairs were documented before treatment.
- Where feasible, the materials used in prior repairs were retained as a form of historical evidence.

Although these points are a laudable point of departure when developing a protocol for considering prior repairs, they do not go far enough. In addition to documenting the existence of prior repairs—ideally with great thoroughness—conservators must also assess their historical and cultural significance before beginning treatment. In her 2003 article on the subject, Jean Portell invited conservators to go beyond the usual assessments for prior repairs (i.e., their chemical and physical stability, their visual impact on the artifact, and the costs involved with removing them). She urged conservators to consider other, less tangible factors as well, because existing repairs may be chemically unstable but culturally significant or may possess historical or spiritual value in their own right (often the case in collections of Indigenous artifacts). Repairs may also have been made by the object's maker or prior owners and should be considered in light of that history.[37]

Portell closes with a list of questions to consider when re-treating an artifact:

- Is the repair aesthetically unacceptable? (Who decides this?)
- Are the materials or methods used in the repair unstable, or has the repair damaged the object? (Does an unstable or hazardous condition require immediate attention?)
- Is the repair documented? (Has the old repair acquired significance as an attribute of the object, to the extent that the object is now expected to match its old description?)

---

[37] One of Portell's case studies involves Christine Smith's treatment of George Washington's will, which had been previously restored by William Berwick. Smith reversed prior repairs selectively, leaving Civil War-era sewing thread and Berwick's paper mends in place while removing stiffened silk and transparent paper mends that obscured the writing. Throughout the process, she worked with the will's present owners and other advisors to guide her treatment approach. Her intensive research for this re-treatment process led to the development of *Yours Respectfully, William Berwick*.

- Was the repair done by a historically significant person? (If so, does this fact enhance the object's appeal or value?)
- Is the repair culturally appropriate and desirable? (Would it be helpful to consult someone who is familiar with the object's culture of origin, such as a member of that group?)
- Does the object, even after repair, have sacred or ritual significance? (Should an appropriate expert be consulted before proceeding with any further treatment?)
- Was the repair done by, or supervised by, the artist? (If so, might the repair interest art historians?)
- Is the intent of the artist known? (If the artist has documented their preferences regarding exhibition and preservation of the artwork, where might one find this information? If the artist is living, should they be consulted?)
- In the case of an electronic or digital artwork, is there a record of a prior substitution or migration? (If the work was reformatted, would knowing what method was used reveal how the work may have changed, and could that information influence a decision about how the work will be treated next?)[38]

Although Portell's questions concern works of art, they are equally pertinent to library materials, whether they are generally recognized as artworks or not. Thanks to Thomas Jefferson's interest in Native languages, for example, the Society holds extensive records and some artifacts related to Indigenous peoples, and these objects would ideally be stored and repaired using materials and methods that their originating tribe or nation deems appropriate. Certain authors (including nineteenth-century minister and novelist George MacDonald) are known to have restored their own libraries. Less famous book owners of all eras have used everything from sewing thread to straight pins to pressure-sensitive tape to keep their bindings together. The significance of these interventions can change over time and may vary from object to object. Without asking the appropriate questions, conservators may remove critical historical context while making a good-faith effort to stabilize a given book or manuscript.

---

[38] Jean D. Portell, "Prior Repairs: When Should They Be Preserved?" *Journal of the American Institute for Conservation* 42, no. 2 (2003): 363–80.

Pre-treatment dialog with librarians and curators is crucial, as these custodians often know more about an object's intangible context: its prior owners, history of use, and cultural significance.

In an ideal world, the conservation history of the APS collections would be readily apparent, and the value of any prior repairs would be understood. The reality is far from ideal, however, as is likely the case at many institutions. Conservation documentation at the APS has been inconsistent, and until recently there was no organized digital archive for any new records produced. The history of previous treatments travelled by word of mouth from one generation of staff to the next, and each conservator apparently retained their own treatment notes. Without Willman Spawn's intervention and Christine Smith's documentation, today's conservators would still not know about William Berwick's and Carol Rugh's treatment efforts. Although it is hoped that more conservation records will be found in the APS Archives, they are currently inaccessible. Processing these collections will help, but the conservation information they contain must still be formatted in such a way that future conservators can use it.

Establishing systems that improve access to conservation records (from file-naming protocols to shared conservation databases to archival retention policies) will ensure that future conservators can put prior repairs in context. Adding previous conservation or restoration treatments to the systems as they are found will help build a history for re-treated artifacts. Historic documents may be appropriately catalogued, filed, scanned, or transcribed for ease of reference. Prior treatments may also be added to conservation databases or spreadsheets for ease of tracking. Knowing who previous binders, restorers, and conservators were—and understanding their materials and methods—can lead to improved treatment decisions in the future, including the choice of whether or not to retain existing repairs. Retaining samples of the materials used in former treatments, when feasible, will provide physical evidence for historic practices and perhaps assist in identifying the previous restorer for a given work.

Improving today's documentation practices will ensure that future conservators possess all the data necessary to make informed choices of their own. Whenever possible, conservation documentation should name any former restorers or conservators, describe their repairs thoroughly, and provide the rationale for the current treatment approach.

What papers and adhesives were used in the previous treatment? How have they aged? What has their effect been upon the original materials? How did their history impact the treatment plan? The Society's future conservators will appreciate knowing not only why an object was treated at a given time but which factors were considered in the decision to retain or remove existing repairs. Stating the goals of treatment and describing the reasons why a given course of action was selected will help put our own choices in context when the objects we have treated need attention once more.

Index

Page numbers followed by "f" indicate figures.